Olgierd Budrewicz

Poland for Beginners

D1003369

Olgierd Budrewicz

Poland for Beginners

Translated by Jolanta Kozak

Wydawnictwa Artystyczne i Filmowe
Wydawnictwo Naukowe PWN
Warsaw 2000

This is a book for beginners – for people whose idea of Poland is vague, or – terrible to think – none at all.

Those advanced in the knowledge of history and customs of the country spread between the Oder and the Bug, are certainly already familiar with all the information enclosed in this booklet, but they can still share some of our reflections on the Polish theme, perhaps not quite identical with their own. It would be pointless to remind the advanced students of Poland of the country's one thousand years' history, and especially of the last War's events. They are well aware of what the '80s of our present century meant for Poland, not to mention such basic trivia as the biographies of Chopin, Skłodowska (Marie Curie), or Kościuszko; they need not be reminded that the Tatras are mountains of exceptional beauty, or that the sturdy Polish bison belongs to the herbivorous family of *Cavicornia* and is a relative of the extinct aurochs. Our little volume should rather be treated as a manual for those taking their first steps in Poland. Many things – perhaps short of such truisms as the fact that Poland lies in Europe (which only a few sneerers doubt) – will be explained here *ab ovo*.

All that is being described on the following pages of this book is the Author's own, highly personal and, therefore, slightly biased, choice. The Author will not try to deny that he prefers mountain regions to lake districts, or that he loves Warsaw more than Poznań – even though his sentiments may be contrary to someone else's. He also confesses that he has followed his own hierarchies of things and events and would gladly exchange a couple of wars for a single Polish Commission for National Education – the world's first ministry of culture and education. Oddly perhaps, he devotes more space to forests, windmills and horses, than to factories, steelworks and shipyards. He is more inclined to extoll the achievements of Polish world-famous restorers of art and architecture, than to fall into ruptures over those who kick the ball or hunt the wolves. Nevertheless, he does his best to restrain himself from any judgement that might easily be deemed provocative.

All beginners in the study of Poland should be warned that the lecture they are about to confront is not only utterly unofficial, but also openly biased (being, of course, exact and truthful on the factual level). It should therefore be dealt with without too much solemnity.

Graduates of our present beginner course are advised to reach for some more comprehensive and profound literature on the subject, since the present booklet will purposefully lack great seriousness, which – please, excuse the Author's complacency – is probably to its own benefit. It certainly leaves the necessity of consulting a broader guide to this country, a longer historical lecture, as well as at least a brief introduction to the scientific, artistic and other aspects of the Polish panorama.

Anyway, the secret truth is that Poland can be learnt only during practical classes, i.e., in personal contact with this rather handsome and quite exceptional country and with its people whose characters, temperaments and life-styles distinguish them clearly from other European nations.

Let us make just one more point. Since June 1989, Poland has been a new country: we call it the Third Republic. We are still in the process of going through a difficult stage of convalescence, following the 45 years of "people's power": it is a period of normalization and general de-stultification of our lives. The transition is far from painless, but that – as Winnie-the-Pooh would say – is quite another story.

Fortunately, certain values will never be lost, as long as the Polish tribe survives in this part of the subcontinent.

Poland, Europe

Poland is close to reaching the magic population limit of 40 million. The country is presently inhabited by 38.7 million, but birthrate is extremely low. According to optimistic prognostics of early 2000, the population may grow to 40 million by the year 2005. Its area makes our country the seventh, and its population – the sixth in Europe. With less than 120 citizens to one square kilometre, there is still ample living space.

Ethnically, Poland is almost homogeneous: only less than one million of the citizens are of non-Polish nationalities, such as Byelorussian, Ukrainian, Lithuanian, or German. It is, therefore, worth reminding that back in 1939, only 68% of the country's population were Poles, the rest being of national minorities, including 3.5 million Jews.

Immediately before the War, Poland boasted a successful modern economy – it is then that the Central Industrial District (COP) was founded and the major port of Gdynia was built, while Polish Airlines belonged to Europe's champions in the air, and Polish Railways were renowned for the punctuality of their trains (memories, memories!).

After the War, the country's industrial develompent was continued by the communists – alas, in a manner, kindly speaking, not quite thoughtful. Many new companies were bound in close cooperation with their Soviet counterparts and some steelworks and factories were literally connected with the other side of the Eastern border, by railways of expanded (Soviet-standard) breadth. Protection of the natural environment was not given much thought. The new industrial giants, which were promptly given the names of Lenin, Stalin and Bierut, have now become a cumbersome economic problem. Attempts are being made to solve it through privatization, or through engagement of foreign capital.

Let us note that the Third Republic is still, principally, a raw-material producer: Europe's number one in sulphur, number two in coal, number four in copper and raw sugar. However, its industrial output is also quite remarkable: Poland is the world's seventh power in ship and energy production, and 20% of the global supply of silver comes from our country. Poland's traditionally strong, though far from modern, agriculture has always been a strong point of the national economy. Even the communists did not dare to introduce full collectivization, leaving as much as 80% of Polish farms in private hands. The privatization of the generally unprofitable state farms is still under way.

Mean economic growth in the years 1992–1997 put Poland (5.8%) second in Europe, following Ireland (7%).

Poland's aspirations to the European Union have aroused great expectations, but also some anxiety, both at home and abroad.

As they say in Warsaw: things look good, but still not quite hopeless.

Basic Facts

Officially speaking, "Poland lies between 49° and 54°50' North latitudes, and 14°07' and 24°08' East longitudes". In more colloquial terms: Polad lies between the Bug and the Oder rivers, and between the Carpathian Mountains and the Baltic Sea, which situates it at one of Europe's vital crossroads (a truth that has often been sadly confirmed by our history).

Poland is a lowland country, with the mean altitude of 173m above sea level. Only 3% of the country's area lies above the altitude of 500 m. The highest point is at 2499m (Rysy Peak in the Tatra Mountains), and the lowest – at 1.8m below sea level (the Vistula delta near Elblag). There are several thousand lakes and some high mountain ranges. Forests occupy 27.4% of the country's aera.

The total area of Poland is 312.685km^2. The joint length of the national borders is 3582km. The country is divided into 16 voivodships.

Officially, the climate is moderate, though temperatures may sometimes drop by as much as 20°C overnight. The seasons may also differ from year to year. Nevertheless, there is little doubt that Poland's climate is better than that of Amazonia or the Spitsbergen, though it is certainly worse than that of Tahiti or Nice.

Polish fauna is popularly limited to dogs, cats and domestic fowl, not to mention the insects – but, with some luck, you may meet face to face with a lynx, a wildcat, a European bison, an elk, a chamois, a marmot, and even a brown bear (though perhaps "luck" is not exactly the word to describe a meeting with a brown bear on a Tatra or Beskidy mountain trail).

Poland is inhabited by 85 mammal and 220 bird species. It is home to 300 lynxes, 850 wolves and 60 bears. Nearly a half of Poland's soil (47.2%) is arable land. More than 50% of all the crops are the four basic cereals: rye, wheat, barley and oats.

Poland is crossed by major international transport routes. Aircraft of thirty different airlines from four continents land at Warsaw airport. Now and again, this country, inhabited by 0.9% of the world's population, becomes the focus of the world's attention – for reasons historical, cultural, economic and, last but not least, geographical. It is certainly an exposed outpost.

A Thousand Years' History

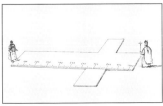

So much has happened on the Polish soil over the past millenium, that the national collection of historical facts would be enough to supply several nations. Whether such a gift would be gratefully received, is another question, as history has never pampered the Polish people.

It all started back in the seventh decade of the 10th century: the ruler that headed the long train of Polish monarchs was Mieszko I. During his reign, Poland became a Christian country.

Mieszko's son, Bolesław Chrobry [the Valiant], was a great king. Alas, a hundred years after his death, Poland was partitioned and remained divided for the next two centuries. Reunited by King Władysław the Short – nicknamed so because of his meagre height, and established as a class monarchy by King Kazimierz the Great, Poland entered a personal union with Lithuania (1385). A crucial event took place in 1410: it was then that King Władysław Jagiełło defeated the Teutonic Knights' army at Grunwald, thus breaking the Order's ominous power.

The 15th and 16th centuries brought a rapid development of grange economy and major privileges for the gentry. In 1569, the Polish-Lithuanian Real Union produced a single, powerful state. The year 1573 opened the period of electoral monarchy.

The 16th and 17th centuries were rich (or, rather, poor) in wars and rebellions. During the reign of the last Polish king, Stanisław August Poniatowski (1764–1795), many attempts were made to secure economical and cultural advancement, as well as social and political reforms (e.g. the 3rd May Constitution of 1792, or the Kościuszko Uprising of 1794). However, the great alliance of the three superpowers – Prussia, Russia and Austria – resulted in the collapse of the Polish state and its partition among the foreign neighbours.

The following 120 years of slavery were a period of ceaseless struggle for independence – a tragic era for Poland, marked by painful sacrifice and a series of uprisings against the occupants. In November 1918, Poland regained sovereignty – only to lose it again, twenty years later (this time for almost six years) to Nazi Germany, closely assisted by the USSR.

During the World War II, Polish soldiers fought the enemy on all the fronts. Pilots of the White Eagle banner were active in the Battle of Britain and largely contributed to its success. Polish troops confronted the enemy at Warsaw, Tobruk, Monte Cassino, on the fields of Flanders and in Berlin. Meanwhile, fighting continued all over occupied Poland. In August and Spetember, 1944, Warsaw Uprising soldiers waged a dramatic campaign to keep the parts of the city they had taken.

On 22 July, 1944, Polish National Liberation Committee [PKWN] – an organisation established (with Stalin's blessing) by the Polish communists, proclaimed its Manifesto on the first Soviet-liberated chunk of the old Republic. The act was followed by the proclamation of a law-defying constitution proposed by the so-called National Union Government.

This opened the 45-year period of Moscow-imposed administration. The system was guilty of many misdeeds and crimes, as well as a general economic degradation and ecological devastation of the country. Two generations of Poles were subject to a major test of characters, demanding great sacrifice – often life itself – especially on the part of the World War II soldiers, the heroes of the armed underground, and the Home Army troops.

The years 1980–1981 brought an outburst of collective anger, backed by a strong effort to install major systematic changes. On 13 December, 1981, the panic-stricken state authorities (who had never been chosen by the people), declared martial law, putting thousands of people in prisons: once again, the Poles had to go into conspiracy. Spring 1989 brought the Round Table negotiations that resulted in the 4th June elections of a new government, with the first non-communist Prime Minister in many decades that was Tadeusz Mazowiecki. It is impossible to summarize a thousand years' history of a nation – eventful, dramatic and full of surprises and absurdities as it was – in a dozen or so sentences. On the other hand, it might suffice to quote the great writer: "And so they lived, and so did time go by," or to echo the poet's line: "We have been there – we are there – we'll be there".

The Political System

The restitution of the Second (independent, inter-War) Republic's place names and symbols at the turn of the '80s and the '90s, was conducted at a truly dazzling speed. Polish People's Republic [PRL] vanished overnigh, the white eagle of the national emblem was promptly re-crowned, the most hated, Soviet-inspired monuments were pulled down and many street names were officially changed.

All those transformations followed the parliamentary elections of June 1989, to the Sejm, and the Senate – the latter having been reactivated after half a century's interval. Actually, the elections were only partly democratic, as two-thirds of the Sejm mandates were still officially ascribed to the old oligarchy. Even this, however, did not prevent the establishment of the first government with a non-communist Prime Minister in post-War Poland and, indeed, in all East and Central Europe. The next, fully democratic parliamentary elections in October, 1991, revealed a pitiful 12-percent public support for the party composed mainly of the former communists.

The new sovereign Polish state, with a generally elected President and a two-house parliament, became a fact. The old, shameful vows of eternal alliance with the USSR, as well as political slogans, such as: "Power belongs to the urban and rural masses", have been eradicated from our new Constitution, which was rewritten in 1997.

In 1995, post-communist Aleksander Kwaśniewski was elected President, by a minimum majority of votes. In 1997, following a four-year interval, administration went back into the hands of post-Solidarity forces.

Poland is a member of many inter-national organizations. A UNO partner, it also belongs to the European Council, enjoys the status of an associate member of the Common Market, and is a European Union applicant. Its recent admission to the NATO, following Poland's membership of "Partnership for Peace," is an event of historic importance. Poland is also member of the Visegrád Group, and of the French-German-Polish "Weimar Triangle" Agreement.

The Pope

He is known to the world as "the Polish Pope". The spiritual leader of nearly a billion Catholics all over the world, he has always remained a great Polish patriot, playing an important political role in the recent historic events by strengthening the Polish people's morale with his verbal and spiritual support during his Potifical visits of 1979, 1983 and 1987. He came again in 1991, 1995, 1997 and, recently, in 1999.

John Paul II was born Karol Wojtyła in 1920 in a small town of Wadowice, not far from Krakow. Years later, as the Metropolitan Archbishop of Krakow, he was made the successor of St. Peter in Rome, elected to the post on 16 October, 1978, to become the first non-Italian on the Papal throne since 1523.

Nobody in Poland will ever forget the news bulletin that followed the momentous Conclave in the Vatican: rational disbelief soon gave way to a general enthusiasm, kissing and dancing in the streets, tears of joy and thankful prayers.

Poland has long been known as a country of miracles. The Roman miracle counts among the most amazing ones.

Illustrious Poles

The men and women whose portraits are framed to be hung on the walls of important public places, or just at home, are "the salt of the Polish soil". The pageant of illustrious Poles is long.

Let us name just the champions: Nicolas Copernicus, Tadeusz Kościuszko, Adam Mickiewicz, Frédéric Chopin, Marie Skłodowska-Curie, Henryk Sienkiewicz. They are the pride of the Polish nation.

Nicolas Copernicus (1473–1543, born in Toruń) was an astronomer, a mathematician, an economist and a surgeon. In his major work, *De revolutionibus orbium coelestium*, he explained his revolutionary, heliocentric theory of the Universe. He was canon of the Warmia Chapter. He also commanded the defence of Olsztyn Castle during the 1520–1521 war between Poland and the Teutonic Knights' Order.

Tadeusz Kościuszko (1746–1817) was a Polish and an American general. He fought for the American independence in the years 1775–1783, and battled against Russia in 1792, to become, in 1794, the Commandant of a Polish national uprising. A great military talent, he also installed a number of political and social reforms.

Adam Mickiewicz (1798–1855) was the greatest Polish poet. He belonged to the Romantic generation. Between 1840–1844, he was professor at Collège de France in Paris; in later years, he also edited "Tribune des Peuples". To help liberate Italy (1848), he created a military formation called the Mickiewicz Legion.

Frédéric Chopin (1810–1849, born in Żelazowa Wola) was a famous composer and pianist. His music like no other conveys Polish national character: Chopin's nocturnes, mazurkas and polonaises are a record of Poland's history, as well as of the sorrows and joys shared by its people. Chopin composed two concertos, 58 mazurkas, 17 polonaises, 21 preludes and 26 etudes, as well as ballads, scherzos, sonatas, songs, fantasies, waltzes, rondos and variations.

Henryk Sienkiewicz (1846–1916) was an author of historical novels. He wrote *Quo Vadis*, *The Trilogy*, *The Teutonic Knights*, and many other books. A Nobel Prize laureate; his books have been translated into more than a hundred languages.

Maria Skłodowska-Curie (1867–1934) was an eminent Polish physicist and chemist, working in France. Professor of the Sorbonne University, she was twice awarded the Nobel Prize. She co-authored theories of radiation and authored pioneering works on nuclear chemistry; she also helped to discover two radioactive elements, polonium and radium.

The list must immediately be followed by another ten great names: Józef Piłsudski – winner of the 1920–1921 war with Russia, head of the Polish state and Marshall of Poland; Kazimierz Pułaski – hero of the American War of Independence; Józef Bem – general of the Polish, Hungarian, and Turkish armies; Władysław Reymont – author of *The Peasants*, a novel awarded the Nobel Prize. There was also the great composer Stanisław Moniuszko, and Ignacy Paderewski – the world-famous pianist and politician. And, of course, Ignacy Łukasiewicz – the inventor of oil distillation method and the constructor of kerosene lamp. And the great traveller-researcher Bronisław Malinowski, and the Polish-born English writer, Joseph Conrad-Korzeniowski, and the composer Karol Szymonowski... And hundreds more.

Speaking of the living great is a risky procedure. Unlike the dead, those whose names have been omitted, might protest. Let us, rather, quote a diagnosis of a tsarist Warsaw constable: "The Poles are a dangerously inventive and gifted nation."

A greater compliment has never been uttered.

The Average Pole

The average Pole's name is Nowak, Kowalski, Szymański, Wójcik, or Dąbrowski. He lives in the city, rather than in the country.

The average Pole is getting older and older, but he is still younger that the average national of many other European states. In 1950, only 8% of the Polish population were people aged 60 and more, while forty-eight years later, the average sexagenarian is still faced with the prospect of another 16 (20.5 for women) years to go. A newborn baby born today stands a big chance of reaching the age of 67.7, as infant deathrate is steadily falling. While the number of endemic diseases has dropped (although TB tends to recur), a new danger of AIDS has appeared. Nearly 62% of the Poles – i.e. about twice as many as before World War II – are registered urban residents.

Polish women outnumber the men by more than a million, and the male deathrate continues to be slightly higher than the female.

Families with many children are more and more rare. The majority of urban dwellers have one or two children. The rate of national population growth has slowed down to 1.6 children per woman (the ratio should be 2.1 to ensure a complete generation replacement).

The average Pole is more inclined to divorce than his parents, or grandparents. Over the last two decades, the number of divorces has grown: while the year 1980 saw 307 thousand marriages and nearly 40 thousnd divorces, 1997 kept the latter statistic almost unchanged, at a considerably lower – 205 thousand – number of marriages.

Polish people's education is steadily improving. Illiteracy, which used to be quite common even before the War (23.1% in 1931), has been eliminated. Every eighth Pole is a high-school graduate, and one in every forty boasts a university diploma.

The biggest share of the average Pole's earnings is spent on food (65–75%). Alcohol is drunk in considerable quantities, but its consumption has been going down: from 4.6 litres of pure spirits in 1989, to 3.7 litres in 1996. The average Pole buys more and more coffee and luxury goods. His appetites are steadily growing: Poland is Europe's second largest market for new cars. Evidently, the Poles have more money than they used to; nevertheless, they like to take credits from the banks.

The average Pole loves to be on the move. Now that he is allowed to keep his passport in his drawer [formerly, it was kept by the authorities] – tourist visas seldom now being necessary, and the Polish zloty having become convertible currency – the average Pole travels all over the world, with the help of about 6,000 travel agencies based all over Poland. "Pilgrimages" to Oriental bazaars belong to the past; nowadays, people go on holiday to Thailand or to the Canary Islands, and many travel on business. At the same time, emigration rate has fallen considerably, from more than 100 thousand people annually leaving the country in the '80s, to a mere 12 thousand Polish nationals who emigrated in 1997.

There is no anthropological norm for the average Pole: he may be dark, fair or bald, short or tall (getting several centimetres taller each year). And – luckily, perhaps – there are no tools for measuring characters and temperaments.

To tell the truth, the average Pole does not exist. Each individual is exceptional, and proud to be so.

Lech Wałęsa

The name is known all over the world. As it contains two letters unknown in other alphabets, it is often erratically reduced to "Valesa", or "Valeza", with the stress sometimes falling on the last syllable [the proper pronunciation being *'Lekh Vah-'len-sa*].

Not only has Lech Wałęsa become an international celebrity, but he has also entered the annals of modern history, to remain there, whatever the future may bring to his public and private cereers.

Poland's President in the years 1990–1995 and Nobel Peace Prize laureate, Lech Wałęsa was the first oppositionist to successfully raise his fist against Communism. The leader of Gdańsk Shipyard workers and head of the multi-million-strong "Solidarność" trade union, he was interned on 13 December, 1981, following the declaration of martial law in Poland. Backed by the strong underground political opposition, he struggled until 1989 to liberate Poland from the Yalta-imposed tyranny of home-bred and foreign oligarchs. Defeated in the next presidential elections, he has not renounced active political life, creating an institute of his own name and a Christian-Democratic party. In the 1997 parliamentary elections, Wałęsa supported Electoral Action Solidarność (AWS), presided by Marian Krzaklewski.

"Solidarność"

This Polish word became world-famous in the '80s. Initially, it used to be the official name of a trade union which turned into a mass political movement.

Started in mid-summer 1980, during a workers' strike at the Gdańsk Shipyard, "Solidarność" has survived to this day. It has remained a trade union, but produced a political rep-

Gdańsk, the Monument to the Shipyard Victims

resentation known as the AWS [Electoral Action Solidarność] Movement. The name "Solidarność" has made history as the symbol of a social impetus that managed to undermine and disrupt the communist order in Central and Eastern Europe. All that happened after 1980 to the east of the Elbe, had started in Gdańsk.

In 1980–1981, "Solidarność" claimed 10 million members. Gdańsk then became the second capital of Poland. Throughout the 1980s, the Union's leader, who was to become Poland's President, used to receive endless pilgrimages of kings, presidents and prime ministers. His name was worn on T-shirts by famous actors (Jack Nicholson), pop-singers, athletes and political activists all over the world.

While this is being written, the historical name of "Solidarność" belongs to a trade union with a parliamentary representation. Having won the elections in coalition with Unia Wolności, the political forces that were born out of "Solidarność" Movement could again form a government, presided by Jerzy Buzek, with Leszek Balcerowicz as his first deputy Prime Minister. "Solidarność" will forever remain a chapter in the book of Poland's modern history.

Foreigners on Poland

Poland has been commented on, in script and speech, for as long as it exists. Whether favourable or not, true or false, the comments were almost never without a certain note of amazement. What a curious country, what an extraordinary breed of man! And what an astounding history! "You cannot stop them from swallowing you up," explained Jean-Jacques Rousseau to the Poles at the onset of the partitions era. " but try at least not to get digested." It seems that Polish people have followed his sound advice.

Their specific national character has always been noticed. Even a thousand years ago, in 1018, Thietmar of Merseburg wrote: "Chrobry's people will not be ruled according to the ruler's interests, unless he practises severe punishments."

Both the Polish virtues, and the vices, have attracted foreign attention. Sometimes a foreigner's reprimand would be received in Poland as a compliment, as was Luigi Lippomano's lament of 1575: "Poland is plagued with errors of heresy, all breeds of religious sects find refuge and safety in this country." We have also been praised: "I often saw in a poorest Polish peasant an original wit that, given the slightest occasion, spouts with a wondrous game of colours," Heinrich Heine wrote in 1822. Some others sneered: "Poles being rather disinclined to work, it follows that they eagerly listen to the news and, whenever they meet a traveller, they stop him and pester him with questions, or force him to accompany them to a tavern." (Werdum, 1670–1672). Polish laboriousness, or, rather, the lack of it, has had various aspects: too often forced to work for foreign masters, Polish people resorted to laziness and sabotage as forms of self-defence – while a keen interest in the world, hospitality and a propensity to drink are hardly questionable Polish characteristics.

The beauty and fertility of the Polish soil has often been admired. "As to Mieszko's country, it is vast like no other Slav country. It abounds in food, meat, honey and arable fields," wrote Ibrahim Ibn Jakub in 965–966. The royal chronicler Gall Anonim added, about 1110–1113: "A country where the air is healthy, the land fruitful, the forests brimming with honey, the waters full of fish, the knights militant, the peasants laborious."

Among the many lofty praises was this, from Cesare Lombroso (1900): "History proves that Poland has evolved spontaneously to become both a bridge between, and a lighthouse for the Slavs, the Germans, and the Orient." Later, especially during World War II, when Poland – to quote Franklin Delano Roosevelt – served as "inspiration to the nations," the words of praise were sometimes translated into actions.

The chief merit extolled in the Poles has always been their military talent: Heine, who so fiercely defended Poland, quoting for the whole world to hear from its national anthem – "And yet, Poland has not perished" – wrote: "A Pole will prove as dexterous with a pen, as he is with a lance, and as brave in the field of knowledge, as he used to be on famous battlefields."

A dangerous tendency to over-generalize is a known fact. Common wisdom makes all Scotsmen misers, all Italians – opera singers, and all Frenchmen – womanizers. Neither have the Poles escaped such generalizations. The most valuable comments have been made by foreigners whose feelings about Poland were mixed, by those who succumbed neither to euphoria, nor to resentful prejudice. One of them was Johann Kausch who deccsribed Poland at the close of the 18th century: "The good impression that a Pole's excessive piety makes on an observer, gives way to the feeling of outrage when you observe the same Pole hastily running away from his card table, to prattle away the psalms." The Author of *Poland for Beginners* has no intention to argue with the critics of Poland; he simply wishes to remind them that all the above quotations, and many other, much more damning opinions, had been self-critically published in Poland, many years ago, in two richly illustrated volumes.

World Cultural Heritage

The UNESCO catalogue of World Cultural Heritage includes eight items located on the Polish territory, namely:

■ the Old Town in Krakow (enlisted 1978)
■ the Wieliczka Salt-Mine (1978) – simultaneously included on the list of especially endangered objects;
■ the museum of Oświęcim Concentration Camp (1979)
■ Białowieska Forest (1979)
■ the Old Town in Warsaw (1980)
■ the Old Town in Zamość (1992)
■ the Old Town in Toruń (1997)
■ Malbork Castle (1997).

Several other objects are on the waiting list, including the Old Town in Gdańsk.

Understand

The Second World War

Half a century ago, you would hardly have met a Polish person who had not lost a close relative in the last War. Human losses were estimated at over six million, which – considering Poland's pre-War population of 35 million – made a tragic world record. Some cities – e.g. Warsaw, Wrocław, Gdańsk – were 75–80 % ruins. Three-fourth of the industrial potential needed reconstruction, and 80% of farmland had not been cultivated for years.

The Nazis practised the policy of extermination on the occupied territories. Their aim was biological annihilation of the nation. In October, 1939, the Germans divided occupied Poland into the so-called General Governorship, and the Reich area (Greater Poland, Pomerania and Śląsk provinces) where the policy of denaturalization was practised, often by terror. Jewish citizens were isolated in ghettos and murdered in concentration camps: Holocaust in Poland brought 3.5 million Jewish victims.

On 17 September, 1939, the Red Army troops crossed the Polish eastern border to attack from behind the Polish Army which was retreating, though still fighting the Germans. The Russian-occupied territories saw mass deportations of the Polish people into the Soviet interior, where they would suffer unthinkable hardships, and often meet their deaths. In reaction to the German homicide, the Polish Underground State was organized: no other country had a resistance movement developed on an equal scale. Beside armed attacks and sabotage, as well as political, editorial and educational activities (including underground press and book publishing, as well as clandestine school and university classes), civil disobedience and boycott of the occupant's decrees became a daily wartime routine. German transports to the Eastern front were regularly attacked, robbed and destroyed in Poland. Partisan troops were active in nearly all bigger forests. Daredevil partisan actions were aimed at German offices and military posts, as well as at Polish traitors to the nation, or some especially hateful Nazi dignitaries (such as SS general Kutschera who was assassinated in a Warsaw street).

The Polish national spirit was invincible – as was confirmed by the plentiful and spontaneous production of anti-Nazi jokes and street ballads, not to mention the concerts and the theatre performances organised in private homes.

The surge of armed resistance in the Warsaw Ghetto – a desperately brave response to the crimes of Holocaust – was one of the most dramatic episodes of the War and occupation years.

The final tragic chord of national resistance was the Warsaw Uprising of August–September 1944, a heroic effort of the capital's citizens that cost quarter of a million of human lives and all but total destruction of the city. Parts of Warsaw had been ruined during the fighting, and the rest was systematically burnt down by the occupant, following the expulsion of all the residents.

It may not be generally known that all Polish universities and high schools were closed down by the Germans throughout the occupation, and clandestine teaching and studying were forbidden under death penalty; no theatres were allowed, either (except for a few Nazi-licensed revue and cabaret stages), nor were any sporting events. No books or newspapers appeared in the Polish language (save for the propaganda brochures and the so-called "reptile dailies," written in abominable Polish).

The dark night of terror continued in Poland for almost six years. It left lots of permanent scars and a lasting wisdom.

The National Uprings

Poland was denied independence for more than 120 years (1795–1918). During that time, there were several nation-wide explosions of resistance: the Kościuszko Insurrection (1794), the November Uprising (1830–1831), the Spring of Nations echoed in Galicia (1846–1848), and the January Uprising (1863–1864). Meanwhile, a series of revolts broke out in the Prussian-occupied region of Greater Poland. The three major Silesian Uprisings (1919–1921) marked the threshold of national independence. Last but not least, the Polish Baykal uprising (1866) was a military demonstration of Polish exiles banished deep into Russia. World War II completed the record with the Warsaw Uprising of 1944.

Each of those armed upheavals against the occupants and the oppressors entailed great national sacrifice. People perished, along with the works of art and the material substance of the country. Enemies have never had an easy life with the Poles.

All the uprisings, even if they were only fought locally, were national in character. Their participants were even women and children, and the sufferings were shared equally by urban and rural communities.

The Insurrection led by Tadeusz Kościuszko was the largest in number and the most dynamic. It was then that the scythe-armed peasants rushed to battle, building a national legend. The 1830–1831 uprising – part of the vast revolutionary wave that swept over the entire Old Continent – played an important role in European events. And the military and social upheaval of 1863–1864 – though it ended in defeat – brought a record number of 1200 major and minor battles. The tragic toll of the 1944 Warsaw Uprising was a quarter of a million dead, and a total annihilation of the city.

These are only the most important Polish national uprisings. But the endless Polish resistance activity was also made up by countless other, more or less important revolutionary episodes, such as the great strike of 1905, or the workers' rebellion in Łódź.

Polish uprisings have sometimes been criticised as aimless efforts, entailing too high a price paid by the entire nation. History, however, seems to confirm the truth that independence is never offered from above, but must be fought for, purposefully and regardless of sacrifice. The Poles have repeatedly proved champions in this mission.

Alexander Hercen – a Russian writer, thinker and revolutionary democrat, one of the noblest characters of the 19th century – on hearing the news of the 1863 uprising, exclaimed: "The uprising has burst out, its flames are spreading across Poland. What will the Petersburg fire brigades do now? ...Gush it with blood – or not? ...And can blood quench fire?"

Hercen, too, wrote about the Poles: "The world cannot deny you its admiration."

This was, indeed, the one thing that the world never denied the Poles.

Sobieski at Vienna

Once upon a time... In 1683, Polish King Jan III Sobieski led 25 thousand warriors to defend the Turk-besieged Vienna. The King later took command of his own army, as well as the Austrian and the German troops (a total of 70 thousand men). The siege was broken and the 115-thousand-strong army of Kara Mustafa was forced to flee from the battlefield.

The victory was largely helped by the troops of Polish winged hussars who attacked the Turks from the hill of Kahlenberg. The flutter of their wings frightened the enemy, and especially the Turkish horses.

The Battle of Vienna put an end to the Turkish expansion in South-Eastern Europe, thus initiating a new historical era.

Some historians have tried – rather vainly – to discredit the feat of King Jan and his men. Such attempts are nothing new: after all, it has long been known that "God cannot change history, but historians can."

The 3 May Constitution

The Polish Constitution – proclaimed on 3 May, 1791 by the Four-Year Sejm – was the first one in Europe and the second – to the American Constitution – in the world.

That important political document was brought to effect at the end of the I Republic's existence, immediately before Poland's subjection to the three superpowers.

The 3 May Constitution confirmed the existing class system, underminig, however, the power of the aristocracy. It abolished the fatal law of *liberum veto* (which allowed for breaking the parliament with a single MP's cry: "I object!"), as well as free elections to the royal throne; the role played by the aristocratic senate was diminished, while more rights were granted the urban middle class, and the peasants were promised "state and legal protection."

Thanks to its message and the literary form, the Constitution document became a major literary work of the Polish Enlightenment. It was an attempt to induce crucial social reforms and to transform Poland into a constitutional and parliamentary monarchy.

The Constitution demanded that royal edicts be approved and signed by one of the ministers. Ministers guilty of breaking the law would have to face trials by paliamentary courts, while politically, as members of the government, they were responsible before the King and the Sejm. Thus, Poland was the world's pioneer in decreeing parliamentary responsibility of ministers.

The 3 May Constitution was abolished in 1792, following a foreign military intervention and the treacherous Targowica Confederacy. Yet, its message survived much longer than did the state it was meant to serve. The Third of May had been celebrated as Poland's national day until World War II, whereupon it was for several decades stripped of the red lettering in the calendar, to be restored in 1990 as the greatest national holiday. Honoured in song and poetry, the Third of May is today present in many street, institution, and public object names.

The Commission of National Education

Founded in 1773, long before its sister organisations in other European countries, it was the world's first ministry of education, in the modern sense of the term.

The Commission realized progressive, secular educational theories, by introducing modern programmes, methods and teaching systems. It reformed the high school and university systems, and was Poland's pioneer in organising teachers' seminars.

The Catholic Church lost its monopoly as educator of the nation. The Commission of National Education worked towards diminishing class differences in education and modernizing school handbooks. It succeeded in establishing the Polish language (instead of Latin) as the official language of instruction at universities.

Many eminent humanists, scientists and social activists – to name only Hugo Kołłątaj – cooperated with that first European department of education.

The Commission of National Education was one of the most powerful grassroot organisations to have ever emerged in Poland.

The Gentry

"All together, gentlemen!" was the outcry that for centuries accompanied Polish history. It was the call of the gentry – that overprivileged social class that became the pillar of the First Republic, shaping the national history, manners and mentality.

It all started with the chivalry, back in the 13th, or the 14th century. The gentry made full use of the law of hereditary land ownership, as well as many other privileges it had forced on the monarchs. There were, of course, different kinds of noblemen: the aristocracy, the "middle" gentry, the farming gentry, and the landless gentry, called *gołota* ["the threadbare"].

Rusticity and chivalry were the two staples of Polish gentry's life. In some regions of the country, members of the petty gentry used to measure their lands by sword-lengths.

Rusticity coloured the gentry's life, manners, and even literature. Writers and poets had for ages succumbed to the charms of rural nobility: "Peaceful country, cheerful country, where's the voice to match your glory" – asked poet Jan Kochanowski. That idyllic picture made an amazing counterpoint to the gentry's political role.

Polish nobility preferred to settle down in wooden country manors. In the borderland, the manors were often fortified to make castle-like strongholds.

According to an old Polish custom – amazing to the rest of the world – family fortunes were inherited by the youngest, instead of the eldest son. The idea behind it was to secure a direct continuity of generations. However, more often than not, fortunes were simply divided among the heirs, in just proportions.

In the early 17th century, Frenchman Guillaume de Beauplan offered this description of the Polish gentry: "Among the Polish nobility, all are equal, unlike in France, Germany, Italy, Spain, etc., where they use the titles of dukes, marquises, counts and barons. A nobleman owning even a scant piece of land will think himself equal to any other, even much wealthier than himself. Each gentleman, the poorest included, flatters himself with the hope of being one day nominated senator by the King. Therefore, starting from childhood, each keenly studies Latin. Each wishes also to become the elderman of his district, the which to achieve, they forever compete in offering proofs of virility and chivalry. It is a known thing that the gentry possess the privilege of electing the king. A nobleman must not be imprisoned prior to his court trial and sentence. Should a nobleman be murdered, the law demands that the killer be beheaded and his goods confiscated."

Long litanies of privileges, few obligations. The gentry were famous for swashbuckle militancy and lavish banqueting. They constantly switched from the saddle (of the royal cavalry, known as "the popular movement" or, since the 15th century, mercenary troops) to the lush banqueting table. The gentry's economic basis was feudal farming, based on forced peasant labour. The system of serfdom made the peasants unpaid labour force and servants to the gentry, in return for the right to till a piece of land.

As the megalomania of the nobility grew, "Sarmatian" manners more and more often took the shape of hot-bloodedness, ruffianism, intolerance, religious fundamentalism and obscurantism. By the end of the 16th century, the gentry had become an undeniably regressive social force. They were responsible for the weakening of the central authorities, the national anarchy and the international degradation of Poland. It was not until 1921 that the privileged status of the nobility was formally cancelled by the Constitution. But the old gentry spirit has not died completely, even though there are no more privileges and nobody struts around in the traditional Sarmatian attire: the echoes of the manners and intellectual habits that had been practised for centuries by that once powerful class, are still audible in Poland. The old principle: "A gentleman's home is his castle," continues to have many unexpected revivals. Whether irritating, or comic, it is still a fact.

Oświęcim

A tragic sound in any human speech. A powerful symbol of human suffering and crime.

The Second World War turned this town, situated at the southern outskirts of Poland, into Europe's greatest Nazi concentration camp.

Some 2.5 million people of more than twenty nationalities were murdered in the vast death factories of Oświęcim (Auschwitz) and the neighbouring Brzezinka (Birkenau). Auschwitz saw the extermination of Polish intellectuals, political activists, resistance members, and especially of the Jewish population (the so-called "final solution of the Jewish problem"), as well as Soviet prisoners of war and the Gypsies. Auschwitz prisoners perished by thousands as a result of slave labour, starvation, inhuman living conditions, torture and executions.

Since spring 1942, mass executions were performed in the camp, mostly by gas, known as cyclon B. Its horrifying efficiency allowed for the killing of 60 thousand people in 24 hours. Two thousand victims would be squeezed into a chamber of 210 square metres. Having sealed the doors, the SS-men would then drop tins containing the lethal substance through the openings in the roof.

Between 1941 and 1944, the Auschwitz camp received and used more than 20 thousand kilograms of cyclon B. According to Rudolf Hoess, the camp's commandant, it took six to seven kilos of the gas to kill 1500 people. The camp was also a scene of outrageous medical experiments. The prisoners were ruthlessly exploited in forced labour factories, e.g. by the IG-Farben concern.

The Auschwitz "death factory" – besides the scheduled holocaust of millions from German-occupied European countries – brought Hitler's Reich a considerable profit. All the possessions of those transported into the camp (and many of them brought in all they had) were looted and stored. Thousands of trains left Auschwitz for the Reich, carrying garments, linen, jewellery and gold, as well as articles of everyday use, such as perambulators, or even artificial limbs.

Prior to the camp's evacuation in 1945, the Nazis burnt down 29 out of the 35 storehouse barracks. The remaining ones, as was found after the War, contained almost 350 thousand complete gentlemen's suits, more than 800 thousand pairs of men's shoes, countless toothbrushes, shaving brushes, spectacles, pots and cups, as well as children's clothes.

Organized resistance started in Auschwitz from the very beginning. It was one of the most heroic chapters of Polish anti-Nazi campaigns. The local people often risked their lives helping the prisoners, and many were arrested and tormented to death.

Konzentrationslager Auschwitz was dissolved overnight, between the 26th and the 27th of January, 1945. The only traces left of that greatest crime of humanity were the prisoners' barracks, the ruins of the crematoria, the lines of barbed wire, the watchtowers and the camp office buildings. What remained was the greatest cemetery in the history of the civilised world. On 27 January, the Nazi death camp was taken by the Soviet Army. The soldiers who entered the camp found seven thousand emaciated, half-dead prisoners, 180 of them children.

Two commandants of the Auschwitz camp, Rudolf Höss and Artur Liebehenschel, were executed in 1947, following the sentence of the Highest National Tribunal. The third one, Rudolf Baer, died in 1963 in a German prison. On Sunday, 16 April, 1967, the vast area of the former Nazi death camp became the scene of a powerful, international anti-war demonstration, marked by the ceremonious unveiling of the International Nazi Victims Monument (designed by Jerzy Jarnuszkiewicz and Julian Pałka, in cooperation with the Italian team of Cascella, Simoncini, Valle and Vitale). The ceremony gathered some 200 thousand people from Poland and abroad. The monument was built off the contributions offered by the former prisoners, as well as governments and people of many countries. The entire camp area was proclaimed Monument of Martyrology. It now houses the state museum of Auschwitz. Oświęcim – like Hiroshima, Warsaw, Katyń and other tragic spots all over the globe – is a graveyard of millions, a document of human suffering and a symbol of the killers' eternal disgrace. A warning forever.

Katyń

Among the names of the towns, regions and rivers that evoke dramatic events in Poland's history, that of a small Byelorussian village is near the top of the list. It has only recently been included on the plaque at the Unknown Soldier's Tomb in Warsaw. At last, after decades of lies and stiffled silence, the awful truth about the crime committed in a Smoleńsk forest, can be openly uttered (though it has never been a secret to the rational and the honest).

In Katyń, Soviet NKWD assassins murdered more than four thousand Polish officers, including several generals, shooting them in the back of the head. It has been discovered that similar executions took place at Kharkov and Tver. Thus, the Bolsheviks got rid of a greater part of pre-War Poland's officer corps. Katyń will forever remain a symbol of human suffering – and human bestiality. Millions of Poles fell prey to Nazism, the facts are generally known, and many of those guilty have been punished. The events in the East, however, were much less public. Since 1939, when Soviet troops crossed Poland's Eastern border, a million and several hundred thousand Polish nationals lost their lives in the prisons and camps of the Gulag Archipelago, exiled to that Inhuman Land. Their bodies are still being exhumed, while documents of the crimes are revealed – now with the help of the democratic organisations in Russia, the Ukraine, and Byelorussia.

Yalta

This resort town in the Crimea saw the division of prey, following World War II. It was there that the victorious Western superpowers gave away Europe's part east of the Elbe to the Soviet Union.

The Yalta Conference was held between 4 and 11 February, 1945. Its main participants were Churchill, Roosevelt and Stalin.

Yalta was followed by the occupation of Germany – but also, in practice, of Poland, Czechoslovakia, Hungary, Romania and a part of Austria. The independent status of Central and East European countries became a political facade: these countries were forced into an unwanted political system, governed by police methods, subject to Moscow's dictate, and isolated from the rest of the world.

The price of Yalta has been paid by the subjected nations. They are now free, but the emotional payoff continues.

The Jews

They had lived for centuries in Central Europe, especially in Poland, and then, suddenly – they were gone: millions of Jews perished in the Holocaust. That unprecedented event in human history took place in the 1940s.

Until World War II, Poland had hosted the world's second largest Jewish community: 3.5 million Jews lived for generations along the Vistula, the Bug, the Niemen, and the Dniestre. Between the two world Wars, Warsaw, with Europe's largest Jewish community, was one of the world's leading centres of Judaism. Warsaw's Jewish population had grown from the estimated 3 thousand in 1781 to nearly 340 thousand immediately before World War I, to remain at about the same level for a number of following years. Half of today's Diaspora have their roots in Poland.

The black cloud of the Holocaust casts a dark shadow on the great subject of the Polish Jews, their history and their culture, so unique in Europe... Many senior Varsavians still remember those April days of 1943 when billows of smoke from the walled-in Jewish quarter in the northern district enveloped the city and dispersed, much later, to reveal only singed scraps of newspapers and books, blowing in the wind.

So did the drama end. Only a few out of the nearly 500 thousand Ghetto prisoners survived the ordeal. Some were taken care of by The Just on the Aryan side of the wall. (The number of Jewish survivors in Poland is estimated at 60–100 thousand; they owed their lives to those who would not be intimidated with the threat of a death sentence on the entire families of those who would dare to help their persecuted countrymen.)

The greater part of the Jewish cultural nad material heritage has perished, both in Warsaw and all over Poland; the few remaining traces were synagogues, cemetries, monuments and works of art. The chief survivor was human memory. And the facts in the great book of history.

In Warsaw's former Jewish district, near the Ghetto Heroes' Monument, a new Historical Museum of Polish Jews will be opened.

The present Jewish population in Poland is estimated at 5-30 thousand (no exact data are available). There are nine regional communities. Besides the Jewish Social-Cultural Society and the Jewish Historical Institute, there exist seven other active organisations and associations.

The Polonia

By this word, in some languages meaning simply "Poland," we refer to the Polish people living abroad. They are about 15 million, two-thirds based in the Americas – yet, a traveller may get the impression that their number is closer to something like a hundred million, as immigrants from the banks of the Vistula, the Warta and the Dunajec, can be met anywhere in the world: the Carribeans, as well as South Africa, and Paraguay as well as New Zealand.

It all began with the first national uprisings and the following waves of political exiles. The second half of the 19th century brought economic migrations.

The US is home to the greatest number of Polish immigrants: they are 6-10 million, and Chicago has become the world's second largest (to Warsaw) Polish community. Canada has 324,000 Poles, Brasil – 840,000, Argentina – some 120,000, Australia – some 110,000, France – some 750,000, Great Britain – 145,000, Germany – nearly one million, and Russia – about 1.5 million.

Of all the estimates, the least exact is that concerning the American Polonia, since it is often uncertain whether a Polish American has still retained some consciousness of his ethnic identity, or has crossed the Rubikon of estrangement, severing all ties with his ancestors' homeland. Hence the great difference in the estimates: while pessimists quote the number of 6.5 million, optimists speak of 9, or even 11 million of American Poles.

Among the most eminent exiles were: Tadeusz Kościuszko and Kazimierz Pułaski, both of them Polish and US generals; professor Ignacy Domeyko who proposed scientific methods of exploiting natural resources and organised science and education in Chile; Józef Bem, a general of Polish, Hungarian and Turkish troops, and commander-in-chief of the Hungarian Army; Adam Mickiewicz, the greatest Polish Romantic poet; Joseph Conrad-Korzeniowski, the great English novelist and Ignacy Paderewski, a pianist and a composer, Poland's Prime Minister in 1919. The names of many outstanding Polish miltary leaders, politicians, scientists, constructors and artists, have entered the history books of other nations.

According to a South American survey, Polish people top the list of immigrant groups who are the most reluctant to renounce their national identities. They cultivate their native language and customs, sometimes throughout four generations. Having maintained close contacts with the land of their fathers, they have been visiting Poland in great numbers over the recent years, since the time the former political obstacles were abolished.

A separate chapter in the history of Polish emigrations are the millions of Polish people who, after 1939, were stranded in the then Soviet Union. A vast majority of them were forcibly deported into the Soviet Eastern interior, to struggle with the harsh climate and inhuman living conditions. Few survived the ordeal and managed to return to Poland; many died, or were killed, and many others have remained to this day in Russia, the Ukraine, Kazakhstan, etc. Efforts are being made to help them back home.

Polish Honour

Several nations are reputed, in critical situations, to cherish honour more than any material privilege or other values, common sense included. This has most often been said about the Spaniards, the Italians, and the Irish. Polish people have habitually interpreted the notion of honour differently from the Mediterranean nations, for whom it traditionally implies revenge. In Poland, honour has been rather associated with selfless generosity, defence of the underprivileged, gallantry towards ladies and group or family solidarity – but also, on different occasions, with a Sarmatian pride and arrogance. In the old days, sabres would immediately be drawn in defence of honour – now it is mostly words (often blunt and loud) that serve as arms. For – to quote from Shakespeare's *Henry IV*: "What is honour? a word." Honour and national pride have always been one to a Pole. More than a hundred years ago, a German writer, Harro Harring, remarked: "A Pole's national pride is amazing. It surfaces, given even the slightest occasion, in princes, as well as in beggars."

Many examples of the Sarmatian sense of honour can be found in the excellent, amazing *Diaries* of Jan Pasek. In the 17th century, Master Pasek defended the honour of the Mazurians against visitors from the Lesser (South-Western) Poland, rather crudely teaching them manners by breaking household furniture against their bodies, and then happily drinking until small hours. It must be admitted that honour in the country on the Vistula often means action – violent whenever the need arises, and sometimes needlessly swashbuckle, ruthless, even brutal. Local patriotisms flourish: God forbid that you should ever offend a native of Warsaw, or of Krakow, by speaking derisively of their cities.

For centuries, even until the Second World War, duelling had been fashionable in Poland. *Polish Honorary Code* – 404 articles compiled by Władysław Boziewicz – had its umpteenth edition as late as 1939 (it has recently been published again, to a general cheer and acclaim.) The fact that duelling was legally banned never seemed to disturb the defendants of honour.

It is sometimes rather difficult to define the limits of insult to the Polish honour.

The Fighting Spirit

In Europe and elsewhere, Poles are considered bellicose. It has also been said that when they set themselves to the business, they carry it out sincerely and thoroughly. There is, alas, a sad explanation of this national feature: for more than a thousand years, the land between the Oder and the Bug had been a battlefield and its people had now and again been provoked to resorting to the arms, in order to survive.

There is a story about a Polish highlander raking hay in an alp, in September 1939, just after the outbreak of the War. A Nazi plane suddenly came low over him and started firing. The peasant lay down on the ground, greatly puzzled at having become a military target. However, as the circling plane kept coming and going, he finally lost his patience and raised the rake to shake it at the pilot. The rake caught on the propeller. The plane hurled down to the ground.

If it were true (which it well might have been in those times of wonder), the anecdote would illustrate a unique case in the history of modern warfare, being at the same time a good example of Polish fierce defensiveness. Indeed, Polish people have seldom attacked first; they dislike aggression. Rifles, sabres, or scythes would be seized only when there was no other way out of trouble. That, once seized, they were keenly employed, is quite another story.

Now and again, at dusk or deep at night, that old fighting spirit is suddenly reborn in a badly-lit street or alley. It is also revived at particularly exciting sporting events. Well, it seems that atavisms die hard.

Distorted echoes of the Polish cavalry charges and the desperate battles of old resound faintly at some of today's rock concerts and football matches.

Hospitality

With some patience and understanding, many Polish vices can be tolerated – unlike, alas, some Polish virtues. One of them is hospitality: that wondrous, delightful, boundless hospitality!

The Polish language abounds in proverbs on the subject: "Receive a guest, and you receive God" – but also: "An ill-timed guest is worse than a Tartar." Visiting and banqueting had been for centuries an important pastime of the Polish gentry. Gentlemen travelled to all the nooks and crannies of the land, regardless of the terrible roads, broken bridges, thinly scattered townships and sparse inns. This explains why so many visitors appeared in people's doorways – sometimes they welcome friends or relatives, and sometimes complete strangers.

Łukasz Opaliński, a contemporary of those times, offered this comment in one of his satires: "Death on him who invented being a host in your own house; it's much better to be a visitor!"

And Władysław Łoziński, describing life in the Poland of distant ages, wrote: "Both the jewel, and the ultimate ordeal of social virtues, especially that of patience, was hospitality – that traditional, ancient gentry hospitality, glorified the world over by foreign travellers who had at some time visited Poland; the gentleman's delight and doom, it was both a great pleasure of rural life, and a source of anxiety, loss and quarrel."

When Zawisza, the governor of Mińsk, called on Jan Chryzostom Pasek in his home at Cisów, while on the way to Krakow, the delighted host gave him a hearty welcome. "I've been to Cisów," recorded later the moved and horrified Zawisza, "visiting Sir Pasek, a shamefully kind gentleman. For three days we could not tell the day from the night: we drank and revelled all the time."

The townsfolk and the peasants tried to follow the gentry's example as best they could. Obviously, while the social class system is definitely over, the Polish hospitality has survived to this day. Seasoned travellers claim that being guest to an Arab sheik is nothing compared to being received in a Polsh home whose hospitality may mean a complete moral and physical devastation.

A refusal of food and – especially! – of drink is taken as a personal offence to the host. And, even though a modern visitor is less likely to be offered the gift of a horse worth 24 ducates, or loads of food to take away – he must on no account restrain his appetite on the premises.

Nowadays, an effective visitor's excuse is the necessity to drive back home. Its effectiveness, however, is mostly due to the fact that, sabres having come out of use, the host may no longer slice the reluctant guest up to pieces, for sheer disappointment and keen affection.

Unreliability

Polish people are very popular with the Latin Americans. "They are so much like us," the Author has been told, "as if they had been born here for generations." What, then, is the main similarity? "That's obvious: for them, as for ourselves, time is an ambiguous notion."

The South-American clearly meant it as a special compliment. After all, we are different in so many respects... It is true, however, that a Pole's attitude towards deadlines, appointments and answering letters has a certain "creative" quality: hence the frequent unpunctualities in time and space and the general disregard of dates, hours, and promises.

A fifteen minutes' delay – euphemistically called the "academic quarter-hour" – is a generally approved Polish custom. But an appointment "mistaken" by several days is not impossible, either. And, even though illiteracy has long been eradicated, letters – especially official – remain unanswered for weeks on end, and sometimes forever.

While appointments and private calls are arrived at with (short of obligatory) delay, and university lectures start with a time handicap, theatre and film performances always begin at exactly the scheduled time. Train departures are, generally, also punctual, which cannot always be said of the arrivals. Polish people are talented improvisers. They never fail in rough-and-ready tasks. Given the last few days to organise a major exhbition, or build a stretch of a highway, they will finish the job just in time.

The often-quoted, dramatic deadline – " for yesterday" – epitomizes the metaphysics of the Polish psychological motivation: tomorrow is far-off and uncertain – just like the South-American *maniana*.

Temperament

Their temperament, mentality, social views, sense of humour and choice of entertainments, makes Polish people akin to the Mediterranean nations. A Pole feels almost at home in Naples, Seville, or São Paulo.

It is chiefly the question of temperament. Polish people are "bathed in hot waters" (hot-blooded) and prone to kindling "straw fire" (a flash in the pan). They never conceal their emotions. Their unusual vitality has always amazed, and slightly frightened, the foreigners.

A prize example of the Polish temperament and vitality, as well as fierce stubbornness and ambition, was a farmer from southern Poland, Jan Stach. When his farm had been cut off from the world by the Rożnowski Reservoir, and the neighbours denied him passage through their lands, Jan Stach decided to construct a bridge, all by himself. He worked day and night, summer and winter, hoisting ruge rocks, joining them with cement, digging the earth and sawing the logs. It took years, but finally he succeeded: his single-handedly-constructed bridge measures 30m in length, 7m in breadth, and 12m in height. Jan Stach's unbelievable effort was awarded in Warsaw with the honourable Bryła Order (commemorating professor Stefan Bryła, an engineer and master bridge builder, executed by the Nazi in 1943.) Mr Stach also became the hero of a famous documentary, *I'm Erecting a Monument*.

However, as a symbol of utter perseverance, Jan Stach is not a typical representative of his nation.

Similar perseverance was shared by those who reconstructed Warsaw after the War. In 1945, a French journalist watching caravans of Varsavians returning home to the levelled ocean of ruins that had been their city, remarked: "There is no force to destroy these people. They are like crocodiles, capable of growing back their severed limbs and broken teeth."

The Complexes

A psychological complex – as masters Freud and Jung defined it – is "a powerfully charged system of emotional associations, usually unconscious."

Polish people seem to suffer from a number of "emotional association systems." Their habitual aggressiveness, for example, may be explained with centuries of troubled existence: for years, living in Poland usually meant fighting. Hence, the constant readiness to parry a blow, bordering on belligerence. A momentary offishness or indifference, which are usually put on to conceal the true feelings or as a form of self-defence, may be most effectively overcome with calm patience or, better still, with a joke and a smile.

Countless devastating assaults and endless hardships, combined with a craving for normalcy, had given rise to the famed Polish principle of "pawn and prink." If means are lacking to buy a new dress, to go on a voyage, or to put up a party, they must be found, even at the sacrifice of pawning a precious possession, or taking a bank credit – for the only thing that counts is appearances!

Polish people manifest an extremely cordial attitude towards foreigners. For that reason, they are sometimes suspected of an inferiority complex. That, however, is an obvious misinterpretation: if there is any complex at all, it is rather evident in an antipathy towards certain nations. In fact, Polish cordiality expresses the proud joy of being a national of a country that has repeatedly focused foreign attention. An unrestrained curiosity about the world is another aspect that encourages the Polish people to communicate with foreigners. Last but not least, there is the famous Polish hospitality.

Corpus Christi

The Easter Week should be spent in Seville, the carnival in Rio de Janeiro, and the Corpus Christi – in Łowicz. On Corpus Christi Day, Łowicz processions gather the local population, the so-called *Księżacy Łowiccy*, in regional dress of delightful, characteristically matched colours. Incidentally, Łowicz folk costumes are almost identical in pattern with the Papal Guards' uniforms in the Vatican. Reportedly, a Polish Church dignitary had once taken a bale of Łowicz cloth to Italy: the pattern delighted the Pope so much that he decided to use it for his Guards' outfits – unless, of course, it was the other way round, with the fashion started in the Eternal City and later imported to Łowicz. Tourists flock down to Łowicz to watch the Corpus Christi processions.

The town of 30 thousand is then packed with cars bearing foreign licence plates, many boasting the "CD" signs. Weather permitting, the occasion turns into a photographers and filmmakers' festival.

Corpus Christi is celebrated ten days after the Pentecost. Its date not being fixed in the Christian calendar, few people – especially among the foreigners – remember when exactly to plan their trips to Łowicz. In any case, May and June are the months to expect the occasion.

It is not only the Corpus Christi pro-

Łowicz, the Corpus Christi procession

cession to the four outdoor altars that makes Łowicz famous. The town on the Bzura boasts a Renaissance-Baroque collegiate church (reconstructed in the second half of the 17th century according to the desing of Thomas and Adrew Poncino), a Gothic church of the Holy Spirit (1404), and several other centuries-old sanctuaries. Other places of interest are: the oddly architectured Old Market (Kościuszko Square) with its classicist town-hall, the neoclassical building of the post-office, and the regional museum.

With some luck, even a weekday visitor to Łowicz neighbourhood may meet a local girl in a wonderfully striped skirt, which is in fact a series of skirts, worn one over another. A truly spectacular view!

King Popiel and the Mice

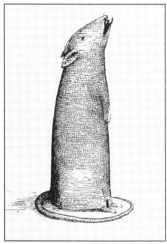

Polish tribes entered Europe's feudal stage rather as latecomers among the Slav peoples. They were the Polans from the Warta valley, the Kujavians from the Gopło Lake district, the five Silesian tribes from the upper and lower Oder basin, the Wiślans, the Mazowszans, the Pommeranians and the Lubuszans. By the mid-10th century, Polan rulers had conquered the entire central area between the Oder and the Vistula. The task of the Polish tribes' unification was finally accomplished by Mieszko.

The events prior to that crucial historical fact had been preserved only in legend. Some of the ancient tales were collected and quoted by Polish chroniclers, like Gall Anonim or Wincenty Kadłubek.

The story of Prince – or King – Popiel is especially fabulous. Legend has it that Popiel was devoured by mice. They must have been an exceptionally starved and audacious breed to have consumed a man – let alone a king. Popiel, also known as Pumpiel, was the Prince of Gniezno, i.e., he came from the very cradle of the Polans and of the Piast dynasty. For reasons unknown, he had been banished from the capital to the place where he was so dishonourably eaten up.

Kadłubek mentioned two Popiels: it is uncertain whether both fell prey to the mice, or just one of them. Finally, *Kronika wielkopolska* changed the events' location from Gniezno to Kruszwica – hence the current legend of Popiel devoured by mice in Kruszwica on Lake Gopło.

Kruszwica is one of the oldest Polish settlements. Traces of an iron-age castle-town have recently been discovered there by archeologists. The famous Mice Tower belongs to the 14th-century castle. It cannot possibly remember Popiel, but it has certainly been familiar with mice.

Master Twardowski

Long before Armstrong and Aldrin, the Moon had been walked upon (or, rather, sat upon) by a traditionally robed Polish gentleman, Master Twardowski.

A Polish Baron Munchhausen, Twardowski survived many fantastic adventures, thanks to his command of supernatural powers: he floated in the air, rode a rooster, turned sand into gold, travelled to the Moon, etc. All that was possible because Twardowski had sold his soul to the Devil.

Master Twardowski, a Krakow citizen, became the hero of many a poem, song and story. From one of the most spectacular and popular Polish legends, he proceeded to enter many other fairy tales.

All the vile inclinations of Master Twardowski were said to have been triggered by his harpy wife. As the old song had it:

A nasty rumour has it that again
Missus Twardowska beat up her man.

Mrs Twardowska was commemorated in a poem by the great Adam Mickiewicz himself.

The Polish language records at least ten proverbs mentioning Master Twardowski, among them are: "Riding like Twardowski on his rooster," or "Master Twardowski on a cock, one foot slippered, one foot shod."

In any case, the unquestioned pre-
cursor of the "pale planet's" exploration was the Polish sorcerer named
Twardowski (given name unknown).

Lajkonik

April Fool's Day

Telling lies on the first of April is neither a Polish invention, nor an exclu-
sively Polish custom. Yet, it is an
important event in Poland, a country
rich in local traditions. An old adage
warns: "Never trust an April Fool, or
you'll be fooled yourself." Despite the
warning, each year lots of people are
taken in, with more or less refined
jokes. The national game has traditionally been joined in by the generally
serious media.

Even back in 1860, the *Kurier War-
szawski* wrote: "Mutual bluffing on 1
April, has been going on since the
beginning of the world. It was on that
day that the devil picked the forbidden
fruit in Paradise and offered it to Eve.
The results still stick in our throats."
The press takes in – and is taken in.
On 1 April, 1930, the Warsaw *Nasz
Przegląd* published a note about
a giant percale factory, founded in
Łódź at the cost of 25 million dollars.
The note was so well edited that the
information was repeated three days
later by the Warsaw *Express Poran-
ny*, with an enthusiastic commentary.
The tradition of press jokes continues.
Nowadays, many papers prefer to pub-
lish trick photography, showing, for
example, a new building erected in
Marszałkowska street, or a double-
headed giraffe allegedly born in the
Warsaw zoo. Initiated in ancient
Rome, April Fools' Day came to
Poland in the 16th century. Let's hope
this piece of information, borrowed
from the encyclopaedia, is not a joke.

Lajkonik

A charming and unique folk entertainment, listed among Krakow's
principal attractions, is *Lajkonik*,
organised on the eighth day following
the Corpus Christi.
The *Lajkonik* tradition is a truly
enchanting local curiosity – a cherished detail of Polish folklore, rooted
in the Medieval guild festivals.
Legend traces the custom down to
a Tartar assault on Krakow, in 1281.
The Tartars were reportedly beaten up
by brave raftsmen of the Krakow district called Zwierzyniec. That is why
the traditional pageants with the
Lajkonik start from Zwierzyniec. The
Lajkonik's Oriental attire suggests its
17th or 18th-century origins, while
the horse's more modern colourful
caparison was designed by that multi-
talented artist, Stanisław Wyspiański
himself.
It would be unfair not to mention that
a similar folk ceremony with a man-
horse has been practised in several
other countries, such as Tibet, Japan,
Italy, or France.

The Sleighing Parties

This old Polish carnival pastime has
lost some of its original popularity, as
winters have become less and less
snowy, and sleighs have been replaced
by motor vehicles. Polish sleighing
parties cruising the neighbourhood,
often in inventive costumes, with
music and song, had once enjoyed
international renown.
The sleighing parties often ended in
an orgy, and sometimes in a calamity.
A crowd descended from umpteen
sleighs would suddenly invade on
a household, gobbling and drinking
up all the food and wine, and abduct-
ing the host to accompany them on
their way to the next address.
Sleighing party members loved to
dress up as Gypsies, peasants, Jews,
priests, or beggars. It takes little
imagination to picture an invasion of
such a groggy horde on a peaceful
household.
Many modern tourist agencies have
included sleighing parties in their
programmes. Alas, with snow, frost,
horses and proper sleighing tracts in
deficit, it is usually an optional offer.

Sobótka, or the Midsummer Night's Feast

On Summer solstice night of June 23rd,
or Whitsunday, this peculiar ritual was
observed among the country folk.
Its magic was believed to secure good
health for the people and their domestic animals, as well as abundant crops.
Sobótka was a giant bonfire, over
which young people of both sexes had
to leap during the ceremony.
Several centuries ago, Jędrzej Kitowicz

described the custom in his *Description of Manners*: "...and especially when the lads, in whose merry company the Old Hornie will always reside, secretly thrust powder-filled keys into the fire. Those, blowing up in flames with mighty salvos, frightened the jumpers so much that, even if they had not entangled themselves in the high-piled logs, they would sometimes drop into the fire, causing their rushing follower, or followers, to do the same; by the time those on top climbed back to their feet, the bottom one would have had his own bottom nicely roasted."

There is strong evidence that *Sobótka* originated as a pagan custom in the times when fires were kindled to honour gods, and jumped over to conquer evil powers.

By the 18th century, the custom had been almost thoroughly eradicated, as a frequent cause of fires and accidents. Some attempts have recently been made to revive it, in order to enrich the tourist offer.

While the *Sobótka* bonfires were ablaze, the girls of old would cast flower wreaths on the river, sending them down with the current. This part of the ritual has survived and still brings crowds of people to riverbanks on a starry Midsummer Night: flower wreaths – symbols of female chastity – are then proudly sported even by the least virtuous lassies.

Dyngus, or the Water Festival

On one day in Poland the consumption of water suddenly soars: it is on Easter Monday. The custom is strictly observed, especially in the countryside. There, the absent-minded and the strangers, ignorant of the danger, may easily fall prey to the wet charms of Polish tradition and custom. *Dyngus*, or *Śmigus*, may be practised in a kindly, elegant manner – by sprinkling the victims with water or perfume – or quite ruthlessly, with bucketfuls of water.

In *A Description of Manners under the Rule of King August III*, Jędrzej Kitowicz wrote: "In town and village alleys, youth of both sexes waited in ambush with hoses and potfuls of water to pour on the passers-by; and sometimes, instead of sprinkling it on a laddie or a lassie, a girl or a boy would perchance shower it on a stranger – a person of great dignity, or a priest, or a stately elder, or an old hag."

There is no escape on Water Festival Day from a lover of old Polish traditions. Nowadays it is, luckily, but one day of the water orgy, but in the old times *Dyngus* could be celebrated even throughout the week. People have calmed down, and fire brigades have become less likely to join in the revelry with their engine-powered pumps.

Kitowicz theorizes that the wet custom started in the times when individual christenings had been difficult to obtain and the need for collective baptisms had arisen. There are, however, many other versions of the origins of *Dyngus*.

Whatever the truth, Polish *Dyngus* is an innocent pastime, compared to, e.g. the South-American ritual of showering one another with barely removable paint.

Folk Art

In this day and age, the most beautiful Indian totems, the most exquisite Congo masks and the most traditional Tahitan fabrics are produced in ... the Far East.

It is, reportedly, also possible to come across a wonderful, colourfully patterned Polish highlander shawl, bearing a subtle stamp: "Made in Japan" – an unusual artifact, no doubt, one of a short series made especially for the Polish Americans.

Poland is still a country of living folk culture, full of God-gifted artists, following the creative dictates of their own hearts. Slowly, very slowly, they are being ruled out, or swallowed up, by the industry. Some defy the prospect of mass production, even at the cost of lesser earnings, while others give in.

Authentic folk furniture, hand-woven cloth, or musical instruments, are becoming more and more rare, as craftsmanship is gradually being industrialized. Nevertheless, Poland still remains a country of exquisite folk art items. There are the universally admired wooden statues, often polychrome. There are the paintings on glass panes. And the much-praised painted stoves and entire houses of Zalipie village, as well as the wood-carved Nativity Scenes from Podhale Region, the embroidered tulles from

Łagiewniki village, the Koniaków laces, or the embroidered tablecloths from the Kaszuby.

In Kurpie Region – especially in Kadzidło neighbourhood – they produce sophisticated, colourful paper cuttings. And many regions of Poland are famous for wonderfully patterned painted Easter eggs. At the roadsides all over the country, but mostly in its eastern and southern parts, stand charming wayside shrines, built by self-taught artists. "Naive art" constitutes an important chapter of folk culture. The names and works of self-educated painters Teofil Ociepka and Nikifor Krynicki, as well as sculptor Leon Kudła, are famous far beyond Poland. A part of Polish folk art can be admired only in the museums. Some items find their way to galleries and shops. And innumerable collectiona of hand-carved saints and devils remain in private hands.

The Museums

Despite the popular belief that all the precious national possessions had been stolen and shipped out of Poland during the many wars, some great treasures are still there to be admired. Polish museums house items of the highest world rank. It may be needless to remind the Reader of Leonardo da Vinci's *The Lady with the Ermine* in Krakow's Muzeum Czartoryskich, but fewer people know that the same museum is in possession of a wonderful Rembrandt – *A Landscape with the Good Samaritan*. Their third great companion, *Portrait of a Young Man* by Rafael, looted during the Second World War by the German occupant, has not been found to this day. Hans Memling's masterpiece triptych, *The Last Judgement*, can be seen in Gdańsk National Museum. Three paintings by the eminent German Renaissance master, Lucas Cranach the Elder, hang in Warsaw National Museum, another two in Sandomierz Diocese Museum, and one more in the Bishops' Palace of Częstochowa. Two Rembrandt canvases (donated by Karolina Lanckorońska) have recently enriched the collection of Warsaw's Royal Castle.

The Bishops' Curia in Siedlce owns the *St. Francis* painted by the great El Greco, but it is not on exhibition. Neither are two other paintings, by the eminent masters Gianbatista Tiepolo and Eugène Delacroix, housed in the castle at Pieskowa Skała. The Historical Museum in Sanok owns a collection of some 600 priceless Orthodox icons, including *The Death of the Virgin* (c. 15th). Poland's biggest collection of Spanish painting, including works by Zurbaran, de Ribeira and painters from the Velázquez circle, is housed in Poznań National Museum. Polish paintings are dispersed among many museums and private collections. Bydgoszcz National Museum owns 700 paintings by Leon Wyczółkowski, while 200 portraits by Witkacy (Stanisław Ignacy Witkiewicz) can be admired in Słupsk, in the Museum of Central Pomerania. Many other paintings, including some by the Munich School artists, are on exhibition in Warsaw, Krakow, Poznań, Jelenia Góra, and other cities.

Warsaw's Zachęta Gallery deserves a separate note. It offers an exquisite collection of modern Polish painting by Henryk Stażewski, Tadeusz Brzozowski, Tadeusz Kantor, Jan Lebenstein, Jerzy Nowosielski, Jonasz Stern, Edward Dwurnik, Artur Nacht-Samborski, and other artists.

There are more suggestions for museum-lovers: an *art nouveau* collection in Płock Mazowieckie Museum; modern sculpture in Wrocław National Museum, with works of the world-famous Magdalena Abakanowicz, Jan Lebenstein and Tadeusz Kantor; a collection of works by Joseph Beuys, one of the fathers of 20th-century art, in Łódź Museum of Art, which also boasts an imposing exhibition of the Polish constructivists; there are Japanese art collections in Krakow and Łódź, and Szczecin offers an African exhibition (including 1500 Malay Dogon culture exhibits). The Diocese Museum in Pelplin hosts Poland's sole copy of the original edition of the Gutenberg Bible, saved thanks to having been shipped to Canada just before the War, and later returned to Poland, along with the Wawel tapestry collection.

Last but not least, there is the truly exceptional offer of Kozłówka, near Lublin. It started as a rubbish depot for the "monuments to Socialism" that had been produced by various artists and "artists" to honour and immortalize the system. When the system collapsed, they were banished, labelled monstrosities, documents of servility, or simply kitsch. Recently, the shameful junk-store was promoted to the rank of a museum of socialist art and instantly gained considerable popularity. For some visitors, it is a grim or pathetic reminder of the past; for others – a memento of what they have been lucky to miss.

The Theatre

As the great writer and theatre expert Adam Grzymała-Siedlecki used to say, "the Poles are incurably theatre-infected." The disease seems to be endemic.

Theatre life has always flourished in Poland. The major theatre centres are Warsaw, Krakow and Wrocław.

Poland has three state theatres: the Great Opera Theatre and the National Theatre in Warsaw, and the Old Theatre in Krakow. Among the total of 125 stages, there are 87 drama theatres. There are 37 philharmonics and concert halls. And a plethora of student theatres.

Many Polish theatres have enjoyed international success, to name only those of Jerzy Grotowski, Tadeusz Kantor, Henryk Tomaszewski, or Wierszalin. Many Polish actors perform abroad, some of them on permanent contracts. Andrzej Seweryn is employed by Comédie Française, Wojciech Pszoniak acts in Paris, London and Lausanne, and director Kazimierz Braun works in the U.S.

In 1965, Warsaw's National Theatre celebrated its 200th anniversary. It was founded by King Stanisław August Poniatowski, and the first head of that important institution was Wojciech Bogusławski, whose statue now stands in Teatralny Square.

The theatre has always been one of the most popular entertainments in Poland. Statistics show that, during an average theatre season, stage productions of plays by the Polish theatre classic Alexander Fredro gather the total audience of 300 thousand, while Shakespeare – the foreign favourite of the Polish stages – attracts some 450 thousand spectators. Another proof of the great popularity of this form of entertainment is the continued presence on national TV1 of the highly-reputed Television Theatre, offering its sophisticated programmes to millions of viewers.

Among the followers of new, experimental theatre forms were the world-famous Wrocław Laboratorium Theatre of Jerzy Grotowski, Henryk Tomaszewski's Pantomime (also from Wrocław), and – last but not least – the cabaret theatres, headed by Krakow's Piwnica pod Baranami. The success of Warsaw's Żydowski [Jewish] Theatre is a source of amazement to many foreign visitors, there being almost no more Jews in Poland and few people understanding Yiddish.

In communist times, Polish theatres struggled with the censorship to stage the best national and foreign plays, including those by Durenmatt and Frisch. Among the other authors were: Elliot, Camus, Brecht, Pinter, Ionesco, Genet, and many more. The annual average amounted to 400 premiere shows, 90–100 of them being dramas by major foreign authors. The growing rank of the Polish theatre was then enhanced by a new, worldwide interest in the avant-garde writings of Witkacy, as well as in the works of Witold Gombrowicz, Sławomir Mrożek, Tadeusz Różewicz, or Jerzy Szaniawski. The names of the major Polish stage directors – Erwin Axer, Józef Szajna, Andrzej Wajda, Kazimierz Dejmek, Adam Hanuszkiewicz and others – gained international reputation. Despite the language barrier, eminent Polish actors have triumphed in theatre centres all over the world – to mention only the great Helena Modrzejewska who set out from Krakow to conquer America. Polish stage design – with names like Tadeusz Kantor, Adam Kilian, Kazimierz Wiśniak, Andrzej Majewski, Józef Szajna, et al. – is ranked among the world's best.

The theatre in Poland has survived all the national crises. It had functioned throughout the 120-years' subjection to the triple foreign power. It was active in Polish prison camps in Germany during World War II. It flourished in conspiracy in German-occupied Poland, whose theatre life was officially banned by the Nazis. The Polish theatre has often been a fighting theatre – as hated and persecuted by the enemy, as it was loved by the Polish audience.

Music

With the din of international pop-music flooding the radio waves and the TV screens, with pop-stars becoming (in slightly dangerous proportions) the idols of the young generation - it is still the *non omnis moriar* for traditional music in Chopin's native land. Poland has not yet become totally

The monument of Frédéric Chopin in Warsaw

Today's Poland hosts many cultural events of international importance. Every five years, the Chopin Competitions for young pianists are held in Warsaw, while international festivals of modern music, Warsaw Autumn and the Jazz-Jamboree, are big annual events. Every fifth year, Poznań organizes Henryk Wieniawski Competitions for violinists. Many other competitions, as well as orchestra, violin and organ concert sessions, attract atrists from many countries.

The Posters

dependent on the modern fashion, nor has it collapsed under the avalanche of decibels.

Musical annals abound in names of great Polish composers and virtuosos. Many modern Polish composers have enjoyed widespread International fame, to name only Witold Lutosławski, Tadeusz Baird, Krzysztof Penderecki, Mikołaj Górecki, Wojciech Kilar or Andrzej Panufnik. They belong to the European musical elite and their music has entered the repertoires of the most eminent orchestras and ensembles.

Among those universally acclaimed are: Arthur Rubinstein, Witold Małcużyński, Halina Czerny-Stefańska, as well as the many laureates of the Warsaw Chopin Competitions. Their high international reputation is shared by Polish opera singers – Teresa Wojtaszek-Kubiak, Teresa Żylis-Gara, Stefania Woytowicz, Bernard Ładysz, Wiesław Ochman, and the violinists – Wanda Wiłkomirska, or Konstanty Kulka. Our symphony orchestras – especially the National Philharmonic and the Great Orchestra of Polish Radio and Television from Katowice – are also famous the world over, and Polish conductors have worked with foreign orchestras on all the continents. Each year, thousands of Polish artists perform abroad. Sir Yehudi Menuhin used to often direct the Warsaw Symphony Orchestra, accompanying it to countries all over the world. The traditions of Frédéric Chopin, Stanisław Moniuszko, Karol Szymanowski, Ignacy Paderewski, Wanda Landowska, Bronisław Huberman, Paweł Kochański, Jan Kiepura and other musical giants, never die.

The national importance of music in Poland may be illustrated by a little-known fact from modern Polish history: during the Nazi occupation, Chopin's music was banned and playing it was punished with deportation to concentration camps.

However great the achievements of the Polish painters, sculptors, tapestry and pottery makers – the poster artists deserve a separate chapter. It is in this domain of mass-reproduced art, whose exhibits may be admired seven days a week, free of charge, on street walls and billboards, that Polish artists have been especially creative and prolific.

Its origins rooted in an indefinite past, Polish modern poster art started in the period between the Wars. The post-War years saw an unprecedented explosion of inventiveness and talent among Polish poster artists. Some, listed among the world's greatest, have made poster history and are now exhibited in the top museums (including New York's MOMA) and reproduced in albums. Among the international poster champions are Polish Wojciech Fangor, Henryk Tomaszewski, Józef Mroszczak, Stanisław Zamecznik, Jan Lenica, Roman Cieślewicz, Tadeusz Trepkowski, Jan Młodożeniec, Waldemar Świerzy and Franciszek Starowieyski. The Polish poster team has won more international awards than any other one in Europe. The Polish artists specialize in many kinds of posters, including political, social and commercial ads, but they are especially famous for their theatre, film and circus posters.

Next door to Wilanów Palace in Warsaw, there is one of the world's few poster museums. It often holds special exhibitions of foreign poster makers.

The Author of this book considers the poster to be the leading form of Polish modern art.

The necessary brevity of the information fed to the beginners in Polish studies, includes only the greatest names in painting, sculpture (see the chapter on the Museums) and the world-acclaimed Polish graphic arts. More examples of success are easily found. In New York and vicinity, a group of Polish artists – including

Rafał Olbiński, Janusz Kapusta, Andrzej Dudziński, Andrzej Czeczot and Jan Sawka – have been active for years. It is a fact worth quoting in the Guinnes Book of Records that as many as 27 Polish artists (most of them now U.S.-based) have been publishing their (especially graphic) works in the "New York Times"!

The Film

When Apolonia Chałupiec – better known to the world as Pola Negri – first appeared in Polish film melodramas of glittering drawing-rooms and shady dives, nobody expected that the Xth Muse would soon make a sweeping career, Pola Negri herself conquering Hollywood and the entire world.

In the years between the two world wars, the Polish film had its ups and downs, mostly the latter. Immediately after World War II, it demonstrated some uncertainty, a little promise, and a few interesting productions, such as *Banned Songs*, or *The Last Stage*. In the mid-'50s, two new names appeared in the Polish cinema: Andrzej Wajda and Andrzej Munk. Wajda made a series of films illustrating the fates of the young generation during the War – especially *Kanal* and *Ashes and Diamond*, based on a novel by Jerzy Andrzejewski. Munk proved his unusual talent, directing *Eroica*, *Cross-eyed Luck* and *The Passenger*, before his death in a car accident, in 1961. The same years saw the debut of Jerzy Kawalerowicz with *Mother Joan of the Angels*, while Wojciech Has, Kazimierz Kutz and Jerzy Hoffman soon followed suit.

An unusual fact about the Polish film--making was the active participation of writers in preparing the scripts; the group included the unimitable Tadeusz Konwicki and Jerzy Stawiński. A new group of filmmakers came with Roman Polański (whose single Polish--made film *A Knife in Water* was followed by the artist's emigration), Jerzy Skolimowski and Krzysztof Zanussi. Their successes were shortly preceded by those of the new animated film makers, Jan Lenica and Walerian Borowczyk.

In the 1990s, the Polish film master class still included Andrzej Wajda and Krzysztof Zanussi, with the late Krzysztof Kieślowski just behind them with his *Decalogue*, and Agnieszka Holland, Jerzy Stuhr, et al. With the Television's support, the Polish film has been making its way back to the world screens. Among those who have entered the world annals of film are Andrzej

Technical Academie in Warsaw

Wajda (*Man of Marble* and *Man of Iron*; the Oscar laureate for general artistic achievement in March 2000), Krzysztof Kieślowski with his Triptych.

Mathematics

The late professor Wacław Sierpiński of Warsaw University was doctor *honoris causa* of nine universities and member of five academies in different countries all over the world. A specialist in the set theory, theory of real functions, topology and theory of numbers, he co-founded the world-famous "Warsaw School" of mathematics.

Stefan Banach – a mathematical genius who opened new horizons to the old science, as well as Hugo Steinhaus and many others, also belong to the past. But the "Warsaw School" continues the traditions of Poland's high-ranking mathematical studies. Five out of the eight currently edited mathematical periodicals are published in foreign languages. Poland has seven university centres of mathematics, and the International Union of Mathematicians often holds its conferences and symposia in our country.

Mathematician and physicist of the "Lvov School" Stanisław Ulam contributed to the construction of the American atom and hydrogen bombs. "Banach space" is a universally known theorem. Hugo Steinhaus was pioneer of the probabilistic method in analysis, later developed by N. Wiener in the US. The name of Wacław Sierpiński is known on all the continents: an eminent Spanish professor, N. Cuesta of Salamanca, dedicated his book to that "Professor who has introduced the Author to the Paradise of Infinity."

Among the many visions of paradise, the mathematical one, admirable as it is, seems especially inaccessible to most mortals.

Recent years have brought a frantic computer and Internet boom in Poland:

it seems that Polish mathematical talents have been shifted on-line.

Jagiellonian University

King Kazimierz Wielki founded this university in Krakow in 1364, when Europe's academies still numbered less than ten, Central Europe having only one – in Prague.

By the mid-15th century, *Alma Mater Jagiellonica* had gained an international reputation as an excellent school of the law, as well as a source of novel concepts in science and philosophy. Soon, it excelled also in astronomy, mathematics and geography. One of its alumni was Nicholas Copernicus. The University has always had many foreign students.

Through thick and thin, Jagiellonian University continued for almost 600 years – until 1939 when it was closed down by the Nazi *Kulturtrager* and 183 of its professors – some of them of international renown – were deported to the concentration camp of Sachsenhausen, where many of them died.

Today's J.U. has some 10 thousand students and 800 academics teachers. The book collection of Jagiellonian Library is one of the biggest in Poland. The Katowice branch of Jagiellonian University has flourished into a separate academy, named Silesian University.

The Batory

Stefan Batory (1533–1586), a Hungarian by birth, was a great Polish king whom military success led deep into Russia.

Before World War II, his royal name was given Poland's prize ocean liner whose two consecutive incarnations have made Polish maritime navigation famous throughout the world, especially for its excellent service and kitchen.

The "Batory" used to cruise between Poland and America, with some 800 pasengers on board (its successor could accommodate up to one thousand people), moving its weight of 14,287 BRT at the speed of 18 knots. Member of the hazardous allied convoys during the War, the original "Batory" had won the nickname of a "lucky ship," as it dexterously avoided enemy torpedos.

The "Batory" and its successor, the "Stefan Batory", had carried more than half a million passengers, before they surrendered the Polish banner to the air-liners. LOT Polish Airlines is a moderately-sized company, equipped with a modern fleet of more than 30 aircraft (most of them Boeings) that transport 2.5 million passengers a year.

"Mazowsze" and others

"Mazowsze" may well be called the world's most popular Polish ambassador.

Each foreign tour of that folk song-and-dance ensemble turns into an important diplomatic mission. "Mazowsze" has won Poland and Polish culture many friends on all the continents.

This state-sponsored ensemble, founded in 1949 by composer Tadeusz Sygietyński, had a keen animator in the person of the great actress and singer, the late Mira Zimińska-Sygietyńska. The ensemble includes a ballet, a choir and an orchestra, and its members are selected from among the musical youth.

"Mazowsze" repertoire relies on folk music, song and dance, especially from Poland's central (Mazowsze) region. "Mazowsze" boys and girls excell in vivid dancing and singing, the girls' famed beauty distracting the attention of the more sentimental Polish-born spectators abroad.

The ensemble is based in Karolin, near Warsaw. The national and international mail that Karolin receives is immense. If "Mazowsze" were to accept all the concert offers it recives, the year would have to number a thousand days.

There are more Polish "ambassador" music ensembles: the excellent southern-Polish counterpart of "Mazowsze" – "Śląsk", and "Poznańskie słowiki" – the Stefan Stuligrosz Boy Choir from Poznań.

The Festivals

Let us say, without too much exaggeration, that hardly a single day passes in Poland without a festival, a competition, an anniversary, a gala concert, a fair, or a parade. It seems to be a global tendency: with more and more special occasions, national and international calendars have become packed to the brim. Among Poland's prize festivals are: the Frédéric Chopin International Piano Competition and the International Jazz-Jamboree, both held in Warsaw, the Henryk Wieniawski International Violin Competition in Poznań, the Chamber Music Days in Łańcut, the International Modern Music Festival "Warsaw Autumn," the Organ and Chamber Music Festival in Gdańsk-Oliwa, the Chopin Festival in Duszniki-Zdrój, the Oratorio and Cantata Festival "Vratislavia Cantans" in Wrocław, the International Song Festival in Sopot's Opera Leśna, and the Jan Kiepura Air and Song Festival in southern Krynica, Żegiestów and Nowy Sącz.

Theatre festivals also traditionally attract crowds of spectators: the Festival of Modern Polish Drama and the Single Actor Festival in Wrocław, the Warsaw Theatre Meetings, the "Malta" International Theatre Festival in Poznań (hosting 50 and more international acting groups each year).

Polish film festivals have lost some of their one-time splendour, only a few surviving to this day, principally the Festival of Polish Feature Films in Gdynia, the International Festival of Short-Subject Films in Krakow, and Lubuskie Film Summer in Łagów. Toruń has recently become the meeting spot of the world's greatest cameramen and their fans who come to the annual Camerimage Festivals.

Among the many interesting folk festivals, there are some that must not be missed, like the Festival of Mountain Folklores in Zakopane, the Festival of Folk Music and Song in Kazimierz Dolny, or "Dymarki Świętokrzyskie" – demonstrations of ancient iron-smelting techniques, accompanied by numerous cultural events in the Świętokrzyskie Mountains.

Following the historical breakthrough of the '80s and the '90s, the Polish festival calendar has lost some items – and promptly replaced them with new ones. Despite the general economic problems, with state sponsorship almost totally withdrawn, Poland's festival spree never ends.

Enough is enough. That, in brief, was the caleidoscope of Poland's annual cultural and commercial attractions. There is hardly an area of social life whose agents would not advertise their achievements and potentials, competing in organizing social events – be it violin-makers, tree-root carvers, or firemen. The most dynamic (and the loudest) are, of course, the pop-singers: now and again, one is tempted to wish for a National Songless Day.

Foreign-Born Polish Citizens

The great architect Henryk Marconi came to Poland from Boulogne in 1822, and a mere eight years later he fought bravely in a national uprising against Poland's occupant. An outstanding master who created many palaces, churches and buildings that are counted among Poland's cherished national heritage, Marconi left this message in his testament: "*Addio Italia, brava e ospitale Polonia, seconda Patria mia, vi saluta!*" ("Good bye, Italy; brave and hospitable Poland, my other homeland, fare thee well!")

Poland has become "the other homeland" to many a foreigner: thousands have made it their home over the centuries, seeking refuge for a variety of reasons. Poland traditionally enjoyed the reputation of being a tolerant country, free from religious persecution and prejudice against strangers, abundant in hopeful prospects for the talented, the hard-working and the industrious.

No wonder foreigners flocked to Poland, and very often they decided to stay. During the reign of King Stanisław August Poniatowski, and in the later years, during the Congress Kingdom, many of them were knighted. Some were offered high credits of trust, which they promptly repaid in abundance – like Christian Godfryd Deybl who was made army general by Commandant Tadeusz Kościuszko.

The immigrants from all over Europe brought Poland a double benefit: they fought and laboured – but also they had children. In other words, they grew into the Polish society and left their own "sequels" in purely Polish editions.

Henryk Marconi had eight children, and his brother Ferrante had nine. The polonized generations followed

Marcello Bacciarelli, Self-portrait

one another, sharing sorrows and joys with the rest of the Polish nation. Nowadays, the Italian name of Marconi is far from rare in Poland: the late Professor Bohdan Marconi was head of the conservation studio at Warsaw's Academy of Fine Arts, member of the International Council of Museums (ICOM) and International Institute of Conservation (IIC); both his daughters work as art restorers in Warsaw. A number of Polish engineers and architects also bear the historic name of Marconi.

Or take the Bacciarellis. This excellent Polish family, started by King Stanisław August Poniatowski's court painter, Marcello Bacciarelli, came from Rome. Marcello left Poland a unique legacy: having created his own painting style, he produced several hundred canvases (most of them portraits); he also served the King as the royal adviser in matters of art, architecture, urban planning and gardening; he initiated the Academy of Fine Arts in Warsaw and helped to establish the wonderful royal art gallery. Bacciarelli was an Italian who used to dress French style, until, following Poland's partition among the three superpowers, he ostentatiously adopted the Polish national costume, including the traditional four-cornered cap. Marcello's descendants fought and worked for Poland. Today's Bacciarellis, in Warsaw and other cities, are actors, lawyers and engineers.

Poland is proud of those "strangers" who remained loyal to their adopted homeland, even at the price of great sacrifices, sometimes even their lives. The complete list of eminent Polish families of foreign origin would fill many pages. Poland's history abounds in hundreds of foreign-sounding names, such as: Bursche, Gebethner, Lenz, Evert, Kolberg, Fontana, Merlini, Solari, Loth, Gepner, Lorentz, Spiess, Lilpop, Brun, Hempel...

The Collectors

Rarely are works of art in Poland passed from one generation to another, many people having lost all their possessions in the wars. And yet, a substantial number of unusual objects of historical value still remain in private hands.

Out of the three hundred Polish collectors of European rank, a hundred (which is rather a large group) are numismatists. One of the "collector kings" was the late Tadeusz Przypkowski, of Jędrzejów in Kielce neighbourhood, an internationally reputed expert on sun-dials; another is Jerzy Dunin-Borkowski, an apothecary from Krośniewice near Kutno and owner of a wonderful collection of Polish medals, coins, arms, manuscripts and old prints, as well as of an impressive gallery of paintings. Poland's major collector centres are in Krakow, Warsaw and Poznań, where the richest collections of the greatest owners (to name only Wojciech Fibak and Wiesław Ochman) are housed. Many famous Polish collectors have died, and many new ones have taken up their noble task. With the re-establishment of capitalism, a new breed of businessmencollectors has emerged, who storm the auction houses, fishing for precious items. They are the "collector kings" of modern Warsaw, Krakow and other cities.

But Poland has also had true royal collectors: kings Zygmunt Stary, Zygmunt August and Zygmunt III Waza were great collectors of silver-ware and tapestries. The Sas dynasty also accumulated a substantial arts and crafts collection. King Stanisław August Poniatowski, a great connoisseur of painting (some of his overseas acquisitions got stuck abroad on their way to Poland, in England among other places), was also a famous collector of cameos and gems.

Some of the leading Polish numismatists are just wealthy enthusiasts, while some others are practising artisans. Craftsmen-collectors have a long tradition in Poland: several decades ago, the country's leading art collector was an uneducated son of a French *patisier*, Gustaw Subier-Bisier. And the news of a recent robbery of a multi-million-dollar-worth collection of post-stamps from the house of a Krakow pensioner, came as a real sensation.

As things are returning to the normal, the arts market included, there is a growing number of robberies in galleries and private collector homes. War-time looting by the occupant and, later, by local pilferers, makes a separate criminal chapter. It is to the noble and daring individual collectors that Poland owes the salvation of a vast portion of the national heritage. It must be admitted, however, that there have also been some dishonest arts experts, working to the opposite effect by selling or mediating in purchases of Poland's national culture treasures: since World War I, sixteen Rembrandt paintings have "leaked out" of Poland, due to their clandestine business. Warsaw's National Museum once organised a sombre, funeral exhibition of sixteen photo prints of the lost masterpieces.

Polish collectors favour the Stanislavian era, i.e. the times of the last Polish king and Napoleon. A vast number of world-famous gold-and-silver-embroidered Słuck sashes are now in private hands. Polish cavalry tradition is also much admired, as evidenced by the many weapon and uniform collections. "Broń i Barwa" associations in Warsaw, Krakow and London, gather the collectors of ancient militaria.

A growing new breed of Polish collectors are those who accumulate arts objects bordering on the kitsch – chiefly pseudo-*art-nouveau* prints and bric-a-brac, funny postcards, old advertisements and posters, fashion magazines of the late 19th and early 20th centuries. An eminent collector of such "masterpieces" is Professor Henryk Tomaszewski of Warsaw's Academy of Fine Arts, a world-famous graphics master.

Foreign Students

Poland's 159 academies (including 12 universities, 30 technical, 39 economy and 19 arts schools) presently teach 8000 foreign students, more than 3000 of them from developing countries.

The majority study at technical academies, favouring mechanics, electronics, construction, chemistry, mining and geodesy colleges.

It is a common phenomenon throughout the world, and yet, overseas students in Poland are a novelty.

Coming to study in Poland, the young people first need a yearly preparatory training. Polish Language Studies for Foreginers – a college functioning since the mid-80s at Łódź University – presently educates several hundred students, most of them from South America (Chile, Bolivia, Argentina, Peru and Cuba) and from several African countries. Łódź is getting more and more support from sister centres in Krakow, Wrocław, Kielce, Lublin and Rzeszów.

Practical command of the Polish language is developed at summer camps for foreign students.

Overseas students share the rights and responsibilities of their Polish colleagues. They receive monthly grants and accomodation on the campus. But life is sometimes more difficult for them, first of all because English-language manuals are in great deficit in Poland. Also, misunderstandings cannot be totally avoided, like the one concerning a group of Chinese students of a Polish Philology Department who were obliged, for a certain time, to study Latin. There is a numerous group of Japanese pianists studying their favourite Chopin music. Also, the number of Polish emigration offspiring coming to study in Poland has been steadily growing.

The total of overseas graduates of Polish academies amounts to dozens of thousands.

Polish globetrotters often tell of unexpected meetings in distant, exotic countries. It is not unusual for a provincial governor in Nigeria, or a doctor in a Peruvian jungle, to welcome Polish travellers in perfect Polish.

The Women

Polish women are famous in the world for their charm and elegance. Their beauty has been extolled in French poetry and in Viennese operetta airs. The names of Mrs Walewska (see: Napoleon!) and Mrs Hańska (see: Balzac!) ring the bell throughout the continents.

Modern Polish girls are certainly no uglier than their mothers and grandmothers. Athletic, raised on a different diet, they have grown taller and slimmer – "all legs," as they say. Foreigners gasp at the "explosion of beauty" in Polish streets.

We have nothing to be ashamed of when it comes to national and international "Miss Beauty" contests.

Other titles to pride of the Polish women are less acknowledged, although it is not unusual for a beautiful girl to enjoy a professional success. Suffice it to say that the number of Polish female professors and PhDs is now close to 1500.

Let us quote some statistics. The Polish female population still tops the male: there are 106 women (116 in

Warsaw and Łódź) to every 100 men. High-school students are 71% girls, but in the vocational schools female students are only 44.9%. Women make up 47.7% of all the university students, and their number is even greater in medical academies (63.9%) and teaching colleges (63%).

We have been witnessing a progressive feminization of certain professions: 81% of the Polish dentists and 84% pharmacists are women. A similar tendency has been noted in other professions. Even the traditionally "male" politics has been attracting more and more representatives of the "weaker sex." In spite of this tendency, women MPs and local officials are still extremely rare.

As the popular saying goes, "the man is the head, but the woman is the neck that turns the head", the role of women in Poland's public life is therefore worth closer attention. Despite the changing times and social customs, Polish males still retain an old-fashioned gallantry towards ladies, including a kiss on the back of the hand at meetings and partings, giving way in the doorway, passing the overcoat, bringing flowers and telling compliments.

For years now, each new young male generation has been threatening to give up the anachronistic habits. Some have even tried putting the threat into practice – but years pass, and as the boys grow older, they find out that their efforts have been futile.

The Tartars

The bad Tartars had invaded Poland and were for centuries its mortal enemies. The good Tartars helped Poland, fighting in King Jan III Sobieski's army and supporting the Poles in their national uprisings.

You needn't travel too far to the East to see a working Muslim mosque and enter it – barefoot, of course. All you have to do is take a trip to Bohoniki or Kruszyniany villages in the neighbourhood of Sokółka, Białystok province. (And a new mosque was recently erected in Warsaw.)

Both the villages boast wooden mosques, built at the turn of the 17th and the 18th centuries, by the local Muslim settlers (the total Muslim population in Poland is now three thousand.)

The Polish Tartars are descendants of the soldiers who fought for King Jan III. Their bravery and loyalty were rewarded by the Polish king who donated to them several villages in the neighbourhood of Sokółka. Years later, a famous local celebrity became Tartar cavalry colonel, Samuel Murza Krzeczowski, the hero of the battle of Parkany.

The Polish Tartars have for years spoken Polish, but they stick to their own special customs, identical with those of Moslem communities in Arab countries. Hand-copied books containing parables and relligious commands are kept in all the houses. Some citizens of the Tartar villages have retained (or, more properly, inherited) the knowledge of the Arabic alphabet.

To avoid any doubt, let us add that the Polish Muslims have never practised polygamy. However, their attitude towards women is much different from the general Polish custom, closer rather to the manners observed in Iraq or in Turkey

Each Friday, Moslem prayer meetings are held in the mosques of Bohoniki and Kruszyniany. They may be classified as precious monuments of architecture, but they are not mere exhibits.

Spreading over the nearby hills, are the cemeteries, full of tombstones marked with the sign of the crescent. The names of the deceased seem to be taken out of Henryk Sienkiewicz's *Trilogy*: Aleksandrowicz, Bogdanowicz... To this day, the most popular given names in the Tartar villages are: Ali, Mustafa, Jakub and Yahia.

Peasants bowing in the direction of Mecca and practising the dictates of the Koran, are certainly a rarity in a Central European village. No wonder, then, that Kruszyniany and Bohoniki are so often visited by Polish and foreign tourists. Many go straight to imam Ali Bajraszewski, a direct descendant of a polonized Tartar family from Kruszyniany. Like his congregation, Ali is a loyal son of both Poland, and the Prophet.

In 1998, the Common Council of Catholics and Muslims was founded – the first such body in Europe.

Apart from the Tartar villages, Polish ethnological curiosities are few and far between: they include the rather small communities of the Karaims and the Old Believers.

The Karaims arrived centuries ago from the Crimea, and their descendants still live in Warsaw area, on the Baltic Coast, and in Lower Silesia. They observe their Turkish-Judaic cultural and social traditions. The entire world's Karaim religious community numbers only 12 thousand souls.

Another interesting religious community are the Russian-descended "Raskolniks," or Old Believers. They are followers of the schism that emerged in the 17-th century, in reaction to the official Russian Orthodox Church. The most radical heretics were persecuted and fled to Poland. Three Old Believer communities are now formally registered in Poland, two of them in Augustów and one in the Mazury province, in Wojnowo, where they also have convent.

The Cistercians

They came to Poland in 1140 and have stayed until this day. Related to the Benedictine Order, the Cistercians have won a great respect and admiration in Poland. Many of the solid monasteries and churches built by Cistercian monks and nuns have survived over eight centuries, despite the many tumultuous waves of civil and military migrations (the latter not always friendly), sweeping over Poland. What is even more miraculous, a great portion of the wonderful art treasures collected in the monastic buildings are still there.

Providence has always favoured the Cistercians. Their monasteries seldom became objects of direct military, let alone artillery, attacks. It seems that the enemy generals were rather reluctant to follow the advice of Cardinal de Richelieu, who had French cannons labelled with the Latin inscription: "*Ultima ratio regum*" (kings' final argument.) Incidentally, Richelieu was for some time the abbot of the Cistercian Order's first monastery in Cîteaux.

There is a chain of ancient Polish Cistercian monasteries and churches, some of them in ruin, but many seemingly intact. As early as the 12th century, monasteries were built in Brzeźnica (today's Jędrzejów), Łekno, Kołbacz, Lubiąż, Ląd, Sulejów, Wąchock, Koprzy-

wnica, Mogiła, Henryków, Kamieniec, Krzeszów and Oliwa. The first Cistercian convent was founded by St. Jadwiga, the Bavarian wife of King Henry the Bearded. Eventually, as many as 40 abbeys were erected in Poland. They functioned until the 19th century, when the Order was dissolved by the occupants. Only two out of the 40 abbeys survived to encourage the revival of Polish Cistercian community, following World War II.

Cistercian-built Polish sanctuaries make up a substantial chapter of European history of art – a fact that is little known in Germany, Britain, or France.

It is impossible to propose a brief list of the treasures amassed in the old Cistercian monasteries and shrines – of the wonderful Romanesque, Gothic, Baroque and Rococo edifices that are dispersed all over Poland, often off the main routes. Which of them should be named first? Perhaps the majestic monastery complex in Mogiła near Krakow, with its early-Gothic church and Renaissance polychromes? Or the wonderfully preserved late-Romanesque church (1140–1210) in Jędrzejów? Or perhaps the excellently maintained monastic complex in Wąchock, complete with Romanesque wings and a true gem of architecture – the chapter-house, opening onto a Gothic-vaulted, relief-covered arcade? There is also Sulejów on the Pilica, with its late-Romanesque church (early 13th century) and a barbican with Gothic and Renaissance keeps and towers, unique in Europe. And the eleven-bay cathedral in Pelplin, with Gothic stalls and the Gutenberg Bible in the local Diocese Museum. And the 110-tone organ in the Gothic cathedral at Oliwa. Ląd on the Warta boasts a precious 14th-century Gothic polychrome, while other early-Gothic constructions can be

admired in Paradyż and Henryków. And how about the treasure-laden late-Romanesque (1207–1240) post-Cistercian St. Florian's church in Koprzywnica?

Leave the trodden paths of the European tourist routine to become a discoverer of the wonderful old Cistercian monasteries in Poland!

The Wooden Churches

Some 200 old wooden sanctuaries have survived in Poland until this day. A number of them are late-Medieval constructions. Their architecture and interior decorations are unique. Here and there, you will see the remains of old mural paintings. Polychrome decorations of the walls and vaults often include local folk motifs. The churches may be Roman-Catholic, Greek-Catholic, or Orthodox (especially in south-eastern Poland.)

In the old times, traditional folk costumes, multi-coloured head-dresses, haversters' wreaths and ornate collars were hung on the church walls, side by side with paintings of the saints and liturgical objects. Three hundred years ago, ecclesiastical dignitaries ofted called the wooden village churches "robbers' dens." The epithet might have carried a grain of truth, especially in the mountain areas, but, on the whole, the sanctuaries were just landmarks of popular local tastes and preferences, isolated from the mainstream of cultural trends.

Polish wooden churches were usually built in ideal harmony with the landscape, to become spectacular illustrations of the local folklore and specific features of the local communities.

Inside these wooden shrines and chapels, one gets the impression of having entered a Lilliputian house. The main aisle (which is often the only one) is usually designed to hold a mere several dozen people.

Although wooden sanctuaries have survived in many regions of Poland, most of them are located in the southeast: south of Krakow, north of Zakopane, and eastwards, towards Przemyśl. This is the Podhale region. It is truly amazing to discover in the 15th-century village church in Dębno wonderful paintings on the wooden beams, the figures of *Crucifiction* or of the *Madonna and Child*, and many elements of the traditional Podhale folk art. In the nearby Sękowa and a little further, in Przydonica, one can admire the miraculously preserved 14th-century sanctuaries with their original polychromes. And the church in Krużlowa Wyżna boasts a copy of another famous Madonna. Its slightly bigger contemporary stands in Binarowa near Krosno, with a splendid 17th-century polychrome decoration, featuring Passion scenes, with the paintings of *Crowning with the Thorn*, *Pater noster* and *Ecce homo* bringing to the mind the finest masterpieces of the Middle Ages.

The fragility of the construction material, combined with the amazing durability of the buildings, must encourage a reflection on the strange fates of inanimate objects. The longevity of the Polish wooden churches is a wonderful paradox of history. Experts claim that the belfry and church in Haczów near Krościenko – a one-time centre of German and Swedish colonizations – is Poland's oldest Christian sanctuary, remembering the times of King Kazimierz Wielki (the 14th century): the church contains fragments of a Gothic polychrome (on wood, of course) and wooden gargoyles in the presbytery.

Sadly, many other wonderful treasures have perished, due to wars, fires and human malevolence. Fire consumed the beautiful church in Lubsza. Many Orthodox churches in Bieszczady have been destroyed. Gone with the wind are the once numerous synagogues...

The Castles

Some 12 thousand of them stood in Poland prior to the Second World War: castles, palaces and fortified manors, residential buildings bearing the military stamp of the battering-ram era. The future of old castles, palaces and country manors is being discussed all over the world. In Poland, the discussion includes the important subject of wartime (1939–1945) and post-War systematic devastation of the objects. Few of their original owners still live in Poland (more have recently started arriving from abroad to claim their properties), and even fewer can afford to keep a classified historical building with a garden. In the post-War past, the most valuable objects were state-owned and were leased to social and scientific institutions, organisations, schools and cultural associations. The "custody," alas, often meant ruin.

Poland's most precious complex of historical architecture is Krakow's Wawel – the main royal residence from the 11th to the late 16th century, a national treasury and a symbol of national culture. With the change of the state capital, at the end of the 16th century, the new Royal Castle in Warsaw took on Wawel's historical role: totally destroyed by the Nazi during the War, it was carefully reconstructed – or, rather, built again from scratch. These two cities are the brightest gems in the national crown. But there are many more remarkable architectural monuments in Poland. Let us name only a few:

Wiśnicz Castle, some 50 kilometres from Krakow. Built in the early 16th century; Gothic-Renaissance, with Baroque fortifications. Seriously damaged by the great fire of 1831, it threatened collapse, until its recent renovation.

Lublin Castle. Neo-Gothic, with the wonderful Gothic Trinity Chapel and 13th-century vaults that served as Nazi torture chambers during the War. It is now a museum and a cultural centre.

Niedzica Castle. Beautifully situated on top of a hill to the south of Krakow; 13th- and 14th-century Gothic; expanded in the 17th century. It is a recreation centre of the Art Historians' Association.

Thanks to painstaking efforts, three other southern castles have recently regained their former splendour. They are the Castle of Pieskowa Skała (30 kilometres from Krakow; 14th-century Gothic; rebuilt during the Renaissance now in the custody of the local chapter of the National Wawel Art Collection; with a Renaissance garden); Baranów Castle (built in the 16th–17th century; mannerist), and Krasiczyn Castle (in Przemyśl neighbourhood close to the eastern national border; 16th–17th century, late Renaissance-mannerist.)

Let us also mention two palaces – in Kielce and in Łańcut. Both 17th-century constructions, they have been renovated and wonderfully preserved. They are now museums.

Our list should be completed with the castles of Malbork, Szczecin, Brzeg, Książ, Olsztyn, Lidzbark, Niepołomice, Niemodlin, Nidzica, Oporów, Pęzin, and many others. There are also the romantic (and precious) ruins at Ujazd (Krzyżtopór Castle), Siewierz, Ząbkowice, Chęciny, Ogrodzieniec, Czersk, Czorsztyn, or Bolków. All in all, it is worth remembering that Poland is dotted with castles and palaces classified as historical monuments that, after years of neglect and devastation, are now being restored as beautiful ornaments to the local landscapes.

Every day, Polish newspapers and magazines are calling for the reconstruction and renovation of many

other delapidated gems of historical architecture that still await their lucky day. Some of those castles, manors, monasteries and churches are located off the beaten tracks – and find it hard to catch up with the quick mainstream of civilizational progress.

With the changed political system in Poland, many castles, palaces and manors have also changed their legal status. They are now being re-privatized and many go back to their former owners. The renovation of some is retarded for want of financial means, while others are too damaged to restore.

Tzaddiks, Synagogues and Kirkuts

Jews had lived for centuries in Polish towns and villages. Many villages used to be 30, 50, or even 90-percent Jewish: some of them were the seats of famous tzaddiks, others – like Rymanów, Leżajsk, Bobowa, Radomyśl – were important centres of rabbinism. Then came the Holocaust. Most of the synagogues and Jewish cemeteries (kirkut) were destroyed by the Nazi occupants, many others were purposefully razed or thoughtlessly demolished after the War, while the rest fell prey to time.

In Łódź, substantial fragments of the Jewish Ghetto survived, along with the vast Jewish cemetery. Other Jewish centres – Radzyń, Parczew, Łomża, Siedlce, Ciechanów, Węgrów, Otwock, Mława, Grójec, Kutno, Włodawa, or Białystok, etc. – were not so lucky: few Jewish traces survived there and the once strong Jewish influence on local customs, culture, and economy, is now all but forgotten.

Gone with the wind are the names of the most famous tzaddiks: Mendele of Rymanów, Elimelech of Leżajsk, Halbersztam of Bobowa, Jakow Rabinowicz of Przysucha, Habstein of Koziennice, the Morgenszterns of Kock and Kalisz, and Mendel of Warka. While the house of Ben Gurion in Płońsk has been renovated, the local kirkut vanished without a trace. Hardly anybody remembers the Jewish settlements of centuries ago in Drohiczyn and Opoczno, or the Jews in Częstochowa, Kałuszyn, Szydłowiec – and even in the Warsaw district of Praga. Polish people encourage the Jews to visit the land on the Vistula, not only in order to pay homage to their dead in cemeteries and places of homicide, but also to rekindle the thousand-year-old ties of multiform cultural coexistence with the local Polish communities.

Half of the world's Jewish population reportedly have Polish roots. The Polish language can traditionally be heard in the streets of Israel. There have been Polish-born members of Israeli government and parliament – a fact that has given rise to a number of anecdotes. According to one, during the meeting at Camp David, Menachem Begin said to Zbigniew Brzeziński: "It's a real shame that Sadat can't speak Polish, isn't it?"

The Windmills

We have seen the end of one of the oldest Polish industries and professions: flour-milling. For 700 years the windmill was a common element of the Polish landscape. As late as 1954, there were still 1012 working windmills in Poland – but only 29 function to this day. Several hundred are no longer used, but still maintained in perfect shape, while the rest are slowly falling apart.

It would be a Quixotic effort to defend the past greatness of the windmills against modern civilization. Hence, the new concepts of changing the function of the winged towers by transforming them into museums or restaurants.

The most famous old windmills stand in Kochanów (built 1787), Lubięcin

Niedzica Castle

The ruins of Krzyżtopór Castle in Ujazd

(1703 and 1817) and Werginki (1784). A specimen dated back to the 17th century has survived in Śmigiel, near Kościan: the village, together with the neighbouring Osieczna, hosts Poland's unique windmill heritage park. Polish windmills are the most numerous in the regions of Wielkopolska, Mazowsze and Mazury, as well as in Kalisz and Lubusz areas. They are usually all wooden. The most popular type, called the "billy-goat", is manipulated by turning the entire bulk of the construction to match the direction of the wind. Another type is the "dutchman" with a moving "cap". There are also ingenious combinations of the two models.

The official 1964 record of Polish monuments of culture included 867 windmills. Their present number is considerably smaller. Unlike the number of our own, private windmills of life at which we charge, Don Quixote-like, day after day.

The Horses

There are about one million horses in Poland, most of them owned by private farmers. The finest specimens are raised in the country's 28 state-owned studs (in Janów Podlaski, Sieraków, Racota, Kadyny, Łobezie, Łąck, etc.): they are thoroughbred Arab, English, Lesser Polish and Greater Polish horses, 200 of them top-class stallions. More and more numerous private studs are being started. Poland also boasts a reservation of the tarpans – dwarfish horses of 1.25-1.45-metre height. For thirty years now, annual auctions have been held in Janów Pod-

laski, known as the breeding centre of the finest Arab horses and frequented by the most choosy horse-owners. Every spring and autumn, lovers of horses and horse-races meet at Warsaw's Służewiec Racecourse.

Polish horses are used in foreign armies – in Italy, Switzerland, and India. The finest ones are sold at breath-taking prices.

As Władysław Łoziński wrote in his book, *Polish Life in the Past Centuries*: "Every gentlemen was a soldier and even in times of peace, horse-riding was the most popular, if not the only, means of transport, as roads were often lacking: horse-breeding and horse-riding were thus of primary importance. Even a gentleman of moderate means would keep several dozen horses." Many years before Łoziński, a Renaissance author, Mikołaj Rej, gave this brief description of the Polish gentry's greatest delights: "a little horse, a little greyhound, a little bird."

Polish cavalry traditionally enjoyed great fame. The mounted troops often won battles for the army. Until the 18th century, the Europe-famous Polish hussars – wings attached to their light armours, glittering helmets and spears – charged at full gallop, to the rustle of their wings and the clangor of steel. During and after World War I, songs were sung about the handsome and brave Polish *ulans*, or light cavalry soldiers. In the 19th and the early 20th centuries, a number of armies all over the world followed Poland's example by introducing cavalry troops. Between the Wars, Poland had 40 cavalry regiments, which bravely took to arms in September 1939.

The Mushrooms

Polish forests have always been full of wild mushrooms, which is by no means typical of the rest of the world:

many travellers from other densely-forrested countries have had their first encounters with wild mushrooms in Polish woods.

Dried Polish ceps [*Boletus*] is an expensive gourmet's delight: a kilogram may cost as much as a good watch. It belongs to the group of foods whose export is strictly limited and heavily taxed – and smuggling dried mushrooms is indeed a daring feat, as their pungent aroma can be smelt yards away. Poland exports wild mushrooms to countries all over the world. For years, the mushrooms were believed to be highly nourishing and rich in protein, to the extent of making a sufficient substitute for meat. However, newer research proved those theories groundless. This, however, did not discourage Polish mushroom-pickers who continue to harvest wild mushrooms for their unique taste and aroma. As is generally known, one mushroom in a soup is enough to make it delicious – "Two mushrooms in the borscht is too much," as the popular proverb warns.

Polish woods grow 66 kinds of wild mushrooms, the most famous being the saffron milk cup, the boletus, the morel and, of course, the champignon. It must be remembered, though, that half of all the mushrooms growing in Polish forests are piosonous species and each specimen should be carefully examined before the consumption. I know people who, while picking wild mushrooms with their right hand, use their left one to support an open mushroom-atlas, with drawings and descriptions of the undergrowth.

Polish mushrooms bear many imaginative poopular names, such as "satan ceps," "grim ceps," "imperial funnel," "retching pigeon," or "naked goose." Following the Chernobyl catastrophe, the world has become slightly less enthusiastic about Polish wild mushrooms, which have been found radioac-tive (they contain caesium). Recently, however, scientists announced that in order to absorb a harmful dose of the radioactive element, one would have to consume more than a dozen kilograms of wild mushrooms. So – help yourself to the Polish mushrooms (and smuggle them abroad)!

The Bisons

The Polish bison fits ideally in the old anecdote about a girl who first went to the zoo and saw a giraffe. Surprised with the length of the animal's neck, its tiny head and graceful movements, the young rationalist exclaimed: "But such creatures do not exist!"

Surprisingly, the European bison – the continent's biggest mammal – lives wild in Poland. Judging by its primeval looks, the cavicorn should rather be walking paw in paw with the dinosaur. The average male weighs about one ton (some XL specimens may be even heavier than 1.5 tons); it has a majestic, horn-adorned head, brown pelt and a big beard. The bison is a typical forest animal. A carnivore, it lives in small herds. A thousand years ago, European bisons lived in nearly all European forests and made popular big game. As a result, by the 19th century they had survived only in the Caucasus and in Poland's Białowieska Forest. By the early 20th century, the bison had become almost extinct in the wild, only a few specimens surviving in zoos and private animal gardens. And yet, even those few proved enough for the naturalists to recreate the lowland bison species and restore the animals to their natural forest environment.

There are now more than 500 bisons in Poland, a great majority of them living in the wild, in Białowieska Forest or in the Bieszczady region. One-third of the world's entire European bison stock live in Poland. Polish bisons are

imported by Britain, Belgium, Holland, Finland, Germany, Switzerland and Sweden.

With the growing number of Polish bisons, a necessary law has been passed – much to the outrage of many ecology activists – allowing for the hunting down of several old bucks each year. The annual costs of supporting the bison population are enormous – not to mention the high costs of the damage the "kings of the forest" do to the neighbourhood crops.

The Polish bisons can be easily observed in the forests, especially in Białowieża.

Hunting

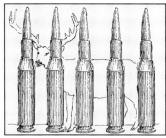

In the times when Poland was still a country of forests and wildlife, hunting was a major branch of economy and the chief means of support for the local people. A mere several hundred years have passed since the days when Polish forests and fields were the huntings grounds for the men, the dogs and the falcons.

Of the hunting parties of old, Władysław Łoziński (*Polish Life in the Past Centuries*) writes: "Falconing, i.e. hunting with the birds, was the most attractive and imaginative type of hunting. More demanding than the other types, it took a lot of patience and money. The class of hunting birds included: eagles, sparrow-hawks, goshawks, falcons, saker falcons, and owls. A good hunting bird cost a considerable fortune. King Stefan Batory did not hestitate to buy a falcon for an equivalent of 120 bushels of wheat,

or a couple of horses, or three fattened oxen."

The art of hunting had always been cultivated in Poland. A truly noble kind of art, it demanded that the hunter meet his wild prey face to face. Hunting demanded quick reaction, physical strength, and, first of all, courage.

Nowadays, hunting habits have changed. With improved weapons and technologies, hunting is still a sport demanding physical fitness, but the element of heroism is almost gone. Poland is still an attractive country for hunters, both local and foreign. The latter, apart from having some command of the gun, must be also considerably affluent, as the price of shooting a bison in Poland may reach $2,000 (depending on the class and kind of the animal), while a Carpatian deer may be hunted for between $100 and $2,000, depending on the weight of the antlers.

Polish hunting trophies are traditionally awarded top prizes at international exhibitions: once, in Turin, the Polish Hunters' Union gathered an armful of umpteen gold and silver medals.

Polish "deer-hunting" is not limited to the sphere of open-air sports. Colloquially, the phrase refers to the dealings of conmen – especially in big cities – hunting for "deer," i.e. naive and ostensibly rich persons. Apart from poaching, this may be the only truly risky kind of hunting left in Poland.

Sports

The Poles are belived to excell in those disciplines of sports which demand courage, quick reaction and a readiness to take risks. Indeed, Polish sailors and glider pilots are among the world's champion class. So are our fencers, shooters and speedway riders. But the Polish judoka, wrestlers, ath-

letes, weight-lifters, archers, speed-boat-riders and canoeists, have also enjoyed great success. Since World War II, Polish athletes have established more than a hundred world records. They have won many Olimpic medals, as well as world and European championships.

Though the present achievements of Polish athletes cannot compare with the pre-War feats of Janusz Kusociński or Stanisława Walasiewiczówna, the names of Kusznierewicz, Korzeniowski, or Renata Mauer are internationally known.

Sport has also become a branch of Polish business. Both playing football, and sponsoring football, can bring big fortunes. Gone is the era of romanticism in sports: now, it is first of all the money that counts. Polish football-players make fortunes playing in many leading teams abroad, so do some famous Polish boxers, etc.

Recently, Poland has begun to make a name for itself in a newly admitted sports discipline, one that requires neither bravery, nor physical fitness, namely, bridge (and, as for bravery and fitness, you certainly need to have steel nerves to stand bidding for the grand slam, as well as a superb physical condition to be able to sit for ten hours at a table.)

Who knows, the encouraging cries – "Knock'im down!" – of the boxing fans, may soon be accompanied by the stage whispers of: "Trumps, you fool, trumps!"

Vodka

Some time ago, the press informed that the Italian prime minister awarded a representative of the Polish "Argos" company with the medal of "Golden Hercules," given to the best commercial products. The laureate was Polish vodka, "Czysta Wyborowa." The award came as the next one in the long line of honours – has it been two hundred sixteen, or perhaps six hundred forty – that have been so far awarded the producers of Polish spirits. In every respectable bar in the world, Polish vodka has its traditional place, next to Scotch whisky, French cognac and Dutch liquor. It is exported to many countries.

In 1975, Polish Embassy in Paris was visited by the then French president, Giscard d'Estaign. As "France Soir" promptly reported, the President enjoyed a drink of Polish "Bison Vodka" – "the lightly coloured and wonderfully smelling liquor based on the herbs of Białowieska Forest – the only place where they naturally grow – which he favours above Polish clear vodka."

It would be pointless to conceal the widely-known fact that the Poles excell both in the production, and in the consumption of alcohol. No wonder Polish vodka is sometimes sarcastically called "eau de Pologne."

It has become a recent fashion to seek respectable patrons for the Polish vodka, making it, e.g. "Mrs Walewska" or "Chopin", as both the protagonists had served their country well. But the brand most popular in the world is now the "Belvedere."

The great poet Julian Tuwim published *The Polish Drinking Dictionary and Bacchic Anthology* – a thick volume containing poems, proverbs and songs. It proves that drinking has always been an important national custom in this country. And the proverb – to quote Tuwim's book – "A nightingale is known by its voice, a thief – by his eyes, and a drunkard – by his nose," has a truly long history.

In the early 19th century, poet Michał Brodowicz advised in the name of all booze-lovers: "Drink moderately, never to excess, and you'll be healthy in body and mind." Easier said than done! Drinking in Poland is not a laughing matter: war with alco-

Krakow, the Wit Stwosz Altar

The Gniezno Portal

holism has been going on for years (and is slowly beginning to yield a certain success.)

Polish vodka is generally 40–45 proof (though some brands are over 70% pure alcohol.) It is produced in many varieties of "clear vodka" and 106 choice brands. The production relies on the Polish potato which is said to possess certain unique characteristics – hence the taste and the quality of the "Made in Poland" spirits.

Visit

The Seven Wonders of Poland

Our opinions on the greatest feats of human intellect and skill may change with time, technological progress and cultural transformations. The same concerns our judgement of natural beauty: some landscapes praised as infinitely beautiful by the Romantics, may now be criticised for resembling cheap, sentimental decorations. But there are, sadly, some tastes that never change, as evidenced by the popular souvenir production, practised throughout the world, from Kalwaria Zebrzydowska to Acapulco, and from Krupówki Street in Zakopane to Piccadilly.

Since the completion of the list of the Seven Wonders of the Ancient World, there have been many rankings of the most wonderful and unusual objects. Poland is no exception to the ambition of recording its own wonders on a single sheet of paper. Authors of such lists differ in tastes and attitudes, and all their suggestions seem highly disputable.

Nevertheless, begginer students of Poland could be advised to start from the following seven local wonders of art and nature (suggestions only!):

Wit Stwosz's Altar in Krakow's Mariacki Church. A masterpiece by one of the world's greatest artists of the late Gothic, this central altar of the archpersbyterial church was completed in 1489. It contains three Marian scenes: the Death, the Assumption and the Coronation. Its perfectly arranged, dynamic sculptures testify to the author's unusual gift of observation, while the wonderful rendering of the figures' flowing robes proves his incredible command of the wooden material.

The Gniezno Portal. The two-wing bronze Romanesque door to the Gniezno Cathedral is among Eu-

Leonardo da Vinci, *The Lady with the Ermine*

The Palace-on-the-Water in Warsaw

rope's finest examples of Romanesque art. Made in the second half of the 12th century by the local bell-founders, it depicts 18 scenes from the life and martyrdom of St. Adalbert [Polish Saint Wojciech].

The Lady with the Ermine by Leonardo da Vinci. A masterpiece by the genius of painting, scupture, theory of art, architecture and engineering, *The Lady with the Ermine* – part of the Czartoryski Museum collection in Krakow – has been equalled in rank with the *Mona Lisa*. The lady in the portrait was probably Cecilia Gallerani, mistress to Lodovico Sforza. The picture was painted in 1490, at the court of Milan.

The Wieliczka Salt Mine. An object of industrial art of nearly a thousand years' history, Wieliczka is famous for its salt-chiselled chapels, salt sculptures and wonderful crystal caves. For more information, consult the following chapters.

Amber. Poland is among the few countries whose soils still contain vast layers of that petrified resin of Tertiary conifers that is used to produce wonderful – albeit more and more expensive – jewellery. Numerous amber exhibits can be seen in the museums of Malbork, Gdańsk and Słupsk. The oldest trade route across Poland was the Baltic-Rome "amber trail" that went through Kalisz.

The Palace-on-the-Water, residence of the last Polish king in Łazienki Park, Warsaw. Partially saved (a sheer miracle!) from the last War, this joint Polish-Italian-French product, designed and supervised by the great Merlini, is exceptional in its scale, proportions and location. Siding with it is the Theatre-on-the-Water, a copy of the ancient Herculanum amphitheatre.

The Gorge of the Dunajec. The spot where that rushing mountain river squeezes among the Pieniny Range rocks. The several-kilometre-long pas-sage is ranked among the most beautiful mountain landscapes in Europe. The list could, and ought to, be extended. This is the task for you. As for myself, I am sometimes tempted to compile another list: of the country's greatest monstrosities. Just like in other countries, it would be rather long. But hush now: the publishers would never tolerate such antics.

The Baltic Sea

It is generally known to be a sea in Northern Europe, connected by the Sund Strait with the Atlantic, and bordered by Denmark, Germany, Poland, Russia (Kaliningrad Region), Lithuania, Latvia, Estonia, Finland and Sweden (though not Norway.)

It is also known to be quite modestly salty (7.8 promille on the average), rather cold and not very deep (the average depth in 86 metres), and as poor in fauna and flora, as it is rich in dramatic historical events.

The Polish coastline is now 524km long – a considerable improvement, compared to the mere 72 kilometres at the outbreak of World War II.

The Baltic Sea has recently begun to reveal its secrets. In 1969, for instance, the wreck of a Swedish ship was discovered in Gdańsk Bay: it may be the "Solen," sunk in the Battle of Oliwa, 1627. It is one of the 200 old wrecks, resting at the bottom of the Baltic. Gdańsk Maritime Museum, housed in Old Crane on the Motława River, exhibits the nineteen 16th and 17th-century cannons that have been so far excavated from the bottom of the sea, as well as numerous other treasures – and waits for more.

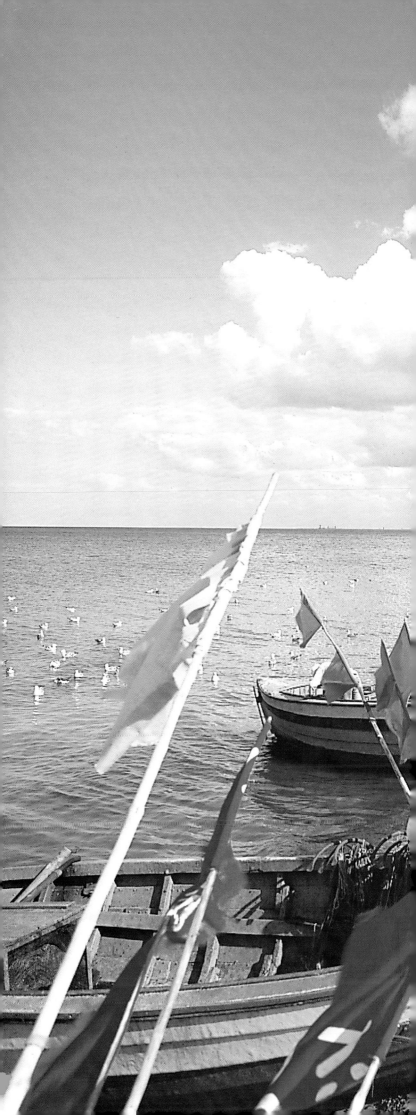

The quicksands in Słowiński National Park

Polish coastline was for centuries a battleground in the wars against the Teutonic, the Prussian, or the Swedish enemy. The area was repeatedly invaded and ravaged, its inhabitants murdered or persecuted. Finally, after several hundred years, in 1945, Poland regained its status of a coastal country.

Alas, the Baltic Sea is also becoming more and more polluted. A cleaning project has been started, as a joint effort of all the Baltic states.

The Lakes

There are about one thousand lakes in northern Poland. This is, actually, the number quoted by the tourist industry advertisers, on the assumption that nobody is going to check the score.

In fact, however, the lakes have been counted: in the lake districts of Mazury, Warmia and Augustów alone (excluding Pomerania), their number exceeds two thousand. Some – like Lake Śniardwy (113.8 km^2) – are so big that you cannot see the opposite shore, while the miniature surfaces of others are often well concealed in the landscape.

The entire stretch of the lake district, still abounding in game, fish and water fowl, borders on deep forests. The largest ones are Piska Forest and Augustowska Forest, filled with a constant wing-flutter of wild ducks and geese, grebes, herons, and even cormorants and swans, also black swans. Still underexploited as a tourist region, the lake district is a popular summer surfing and sailing area, while ice-boaters visit it in winter. In view of its vast tourist potential, the present, rather meagre, accommodation facilities are being hastily improved.

The Warmia and Mazury Region has had a dramatic past, marked by the centuries-long struggle with the cunning Teutonic Knights' policy, and the local populations' stubborn efforts to resist germanization. Grunwald –

a village 50 kilometres from Olsztyn – became in 1410 the site of a decisive victory won by the Polish King Władysław Jagiełło over the Teutonic Knights' army – a turning point in Central European history.

The forests and the lakes are full of treasures. In Święta Lipka, you may visit a Baroque monastic complex with a church, while Reszel and Lidzbark boast Gothic sanctuaries and castles. There are many more to see.

Olsztyn itself – a 14th-century town, picturesquely situated on the Łyna River – is the cultural centre of Warmia-Mazury, certainly worth visiting.

Annexed to Poland in 1454 with the entire Warmia region, Olsztyn had remained a Polish town until 1772, when the First Partition became a fact. In the years 1516–1519, the local Chapter was administered by Nicolas Copernicus who also organised the defence of the stronghold against the Teutonic Knights in 1521. In the 19th and the 20th centuries, Olsztyn was the centre of the Polish resistance against germanization. In 1945, the city was 50-percent destroyed. Today – following years of reconstruction and development – it is more than twice as big as before the War, with a population of 166 thousand.

The 14th-century Gothic castle now houses the Mazurskie Muzeum (with an exhibition of pre-Teutonic local culture, traditional Mazurian tiles, Medieval sculpture, etc.); the sundial in the arcade is said to have been designed by Copernicus. In nearby Kołłątaj Street stands a wooden cornhouse, dated back to the 17th or the 18th century. Other objects of interest include: the Tall Gate (c. 14th), the late-Gothic cathedral (c. 15th), and the renovated tenant houses in the market-square.

Anglers flock to their Mazury paradise in Mikołajki and Ruciane areas, while

canoers prefer the whereabouts of Mrągowo, Sorkwitów and Ełk. The entire lake district has hosts of fans, delighted at having discovered this vast area of calm and clear air. Despite the growing number of motor-vehicles from all over Europe – but mostly from Germany and Sweden – the great blue heron and the black swan have not yet quit the neighbourhood.

The Mountains

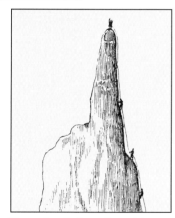

The entire darker-coloured bottom area on the map of Poland depicts a sequel to the Alps known as the Carpathian Mountains. Experts say – and we choose to believe them – that the range was formed some 30 million years ago.

Poland offers a rich sample of the Carpathians' natural diversity. The most exceptional among the range's units of separate rock formation are the Tatras – mountains of a noble, severe beauty. Though far from being of record height (with the tallest peak at 2663 metres), the Tatras make the local sky-line look especially threatening and imposing at this spot of Europe.

Certain sections of the Polish Carpathians have been traditionally referred to by separate names. Thus, there are the many Beskids (Śląski, Wysoki, Żywiecki, Wyspowy, Średni, Mały, Sądecki, Niski, Gorce), the Pieniny and the Bieszczady. North of the Tatra range,

lies a sprawling valley known as Podhale, inhabited by sturdy, gifted and hard-working people. The highlanders build their houses at the altitudes up to 1000 metres. They live off farming the rather poor local soils in the valleys and on the mountain-slopes, and shepherding.

Podhale makes an important and sentimental chapter in the Polish book. The local folk culture has inspired all disciplines of Polish art. The proud tradition of the Podhale Brigade (famously brave during the last War) is still continued by the modern troops wearing special uniforms, with regional highlander cloaks and hats. Mountain folk tunes are sung all over the country, and the local architecture, furniture and costumes are widely admired. Every child knows the legends of the just robbers of Podhale, fighting tyranny and the greed of the rich. Tales of brown bears roaming the mountain trails are also popular.

A peaceful invasion of tourists and sanatorium patients has been continuing for decades in the Podhale region: throughout the summer – and, in the higher areas, for ten months a year – all spare rooms and sheds in the villages that have grown along the valleys and the streams, are hired by holidaymakers. Some of them cultivate their tans in the UV-plus sun, others practise skiing, snow conditions permitting (more often than not, they do), while the rest sip the mineral waters from the local springs. And all enjoy being part of the mountain folk life, cheerfully dismissing the derisive epithet of *ceper* – a milder local equivalent of the American "gringo."

It is advisable to stray from the main paths and visit, e.g., Sądecka Valley, with its really old town of Stary Sącz and an ocean of fruit-bearing orchards; or wander eastwards, to the neighbourhood of Krynica and Gorlice, to admire small village Orthodox and

The Pieniny Mountains, rafts coming down the gorge of the Dunajec

The Lake Morskie Oko in Tatra Mountains

Catholic churches; or climb the thickly wooded slopes of Babia Góra.

In 1905, all those sights met the eye of Samuel Bredetzky, on his way to the post as chief supervisor of the Evangelical congregations in the region known as "double Galicia." Despite his Slav-sounding name, Bredetzky was a German, a loyal admirer of the Emperor Franz Joseph. A foreign civil servant in an occupied country, he nevertheless liked the Poles and spoke of them in friendly terms. As a traveller sensitive to natural charms, he adored the mountains, the gorges and the streams, and left a wonderful description of a sunrise over a golden-lit Mount Krywań. He praised the roads in the neighbourhood of Nowy Targ, but admitted that, further on, the tract became "somewhat worse." The coach rattled and bumped on the rubble, or sunk in the stream-flooded bogs, until, near Myślenice, the desperate driver refused to go on. As the hapless preacher later wrote in his diary, it was himself who gave in to panic and ordered the driver to stop the coach. He descended and hid in the bushes. When he calmed down, he walked to Myślenice, and on, to the "truly regal" Krakow.

Such adventures of 150 years ago can hardly befall a modern tourist, not so prone to fits of uncontrolled panic. Rivers need not be forded any longer, and roadside hostels and inns are in abundance. Only the landscapes have remained as beautiful and intriguing as in the old times – in Podhale, and throughout the Polish Carpathians. It may have taken 30 million years, but it was certainly worth wating for!

The Vistula

This river, crossing Poland from the south to the north, is a crucial symbol of the national consciousness. Reflecting the nature of the local inhabitants, the Vistula runs its course with a leisurly dignity, spreading wide, unrestrained by forceps of concrete banks – which, alas, makes it prone to violent surges and sweeping floods. The Vistula is slowly drying out. Like many other rivers in the world, it is also more and more polluted, causing its fish to seek other waters. Still, it has retained some of its old splendour, of the times when it meandered through the dense wilderness that used to be Poland.

The river's springs are on the slopes of Barania Góra, and its estuary opens near Gdańsk. The Vistula measures 1047km, with a river basin of nearly $200km^2$. It is navigable almost all along its course (941km) – unless, of course, it dries out in mid-summer, or becomes frozen in winter. The major Polish cities on the Vistula are: Krakow, Warsaw, Płock, Toruń and Gdańsk.

The River Vistula flows in the Polish national anthem and in thousands of other hymns, songs and poems.

Flows the Vistula, flows,
Across the Polish soils...

It has been an object of admiration, love and nostalgy.

It has also been witness to many a crucial historical event, and, especially, to many bloody battles that were fought on its bank-turned-frontlines. For ages, it has given this country its tone and colour.

No wonder, then, that it is from the Vistula waves that the legendary Mermaid emerged – a girl-fish, armed with a sword and a shield. Charming and threatening, tempting and vengeful – she became the emblem of Warsaw.

The Vistula brings to the mind small, domestic pleasures, like walking along the river-bank, crossing a bridge, catching a carp – but also fundamental questions of greatest importance:

Hush now, hush, forget your sorrows,
See the flowing Vistula waves;
As they never will cease flowing,
So will Poland never perish.

The lines of a 19th-century poet, Teofil Lenartowicz, depicting River Vistula as the essence of the national effort, are confirmed by the Polish people's general feeling about their native master-river. For ages, the Vistula has been the measure of values and objects; its name is quoted in many a proverb – like the famous: "Crazy fool, the Vistula's on fire!" used to describe a person out of control, or: "Not until Turkish horses come to drink from the Vistula," meaning: "Never in your life." Thus, the Vistula has also become a measure of the absurd.

And what is all the big fuss about? About a river six times shorter than the Amazon, and four times shorter than the Niger, or the Lena?

Well, the Vistula is not just a river, to be measured in kilometres and galons. "The Vistula," to quote the poet Światopełk Karpiński, "flows out of the night and into the day."

The Oder

This river is more than just a geographical item: it is an important historical symbol, tracing 176km of Poland's western national border. 742 of the Oder's 854km flow in Poland. The river is fit for drifting and navigation almost throughout its course, along the distance of 711km.

The regions bordering on the Oder – the Baltic Coast, Lubuska County and Lower Silesia – are famous for wonderful landscapes, as well as economic and cultural achievements. It is on the Oder that the cities of Szczecin, Zielona Góra, Wrocław, Brzeg and Opole lie.

The entire area – including Pomerania and a fragment of the historical Prussia – has been reclaimed by the Slav people, following many centuries of Prussian and German rule. Today's western Poland was originally ruled by the dukes of the Piast dynasty (Silesian and West-Pomeranian Piast families.)

Visitors to this region will never be bored. The Karkonosze Mountains and the Lubusz region are famously attractive resort areas. Kłodzka Valley, the towns of Nysa, Opole, Brzeg, Wrocław, Jelena Góra and suburbs, Łagów and its many lakes, Szczecin and the entire Szczecin Basin, down to Świnoujście – this is just a brief sketch of a suggested several-week-long tour. The roads are usually good and accommodation is no problem.

In 1997, the Oder overflew in a terrible "flood of the century," depriving many families of their homes. A year later, the tragedy happened again, though on a smaller scale.

Thirty kilometres south of the border town of Zgorzelec, lies a geo-political curiosity, called "Turoszów Sack" – a tiny stretch of land, squeezed in between the Czech and Germany, with huge opencast brown coal mines (Turów I and Turów II), producing two-thirds of the Polish brown coal. It is also the location of the country's biggest power-plant (2000MW). Now doubt, the unquestionable technological progress is also a source of harm to the natural environment.

Warsaw

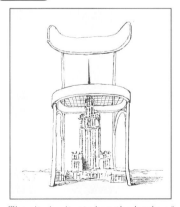

The city is situated on the banks of one of the last romantically unkempt rivers in Europe. Its emblem is the Mermaid – a girl-fish, with a raised sword. The 1,700 thousand Warsaw

citizens are, on the whole, temperamental and imaginative.

The city is certainly worth observing and understanding. It is a city of busy streets, historic palaces, churches, monuments, lovely promenades and parks. A city of sensational history and controversial character.

Being Poland's political and administrative centre, Warsaw is also – and foremost – the national capital of cultural life. There are 18 theatres, giving 90 première shows a year – but also street music-bands and local folk singers. There are major international festivals, conferences and exhibitions – as well as crowded cafés and pubs. There are more than a dozen academies and several dozen research institutes – but also a new, sarcastic jokes every day, commenting on the recent events. There are respectable museums, sanctuaries and monuments – side by side with the living, attractive, ethnic urban reality.

The name of Warsaw rings with pathos and poetry. The city's uniqueness ensues from its martial past, and the iternational prestige of Warsaw's capitals rests on the selfless courage of its citizens, demonstrated in the many wars and uprisings that repeatedly swept over the city roofs and cobblestones.

More than 700 years of Warsaw's history was a period of many disasters, most of them bearing the stamp of Mars, the god of war. At least thrice was the city erased from the maps of Europe: following the Swedish Wars in the 17th century; then, partly, during the Kościusko Uprising in the late 18th century, and finally – and most terribly – at the end of World War II. The events of 1939 and 1944, turned Poland's capital into a desert. Some 800 thousand citizens were killed. There was the Ghetto Uprising (1943), and the Warsaw Uprising (1944). The population of left-bank Warsaw was reduced almost to zero – an unprecedented, grim record in human history.

Today's official records list 917 historic objects in Warsaw, some of them (like the palace-and-park complexes in Łazienki and Wilanów, or the Old Town) calssified at the top of the international list of world cultural heritage. Unofficially, however, the city on the Vistula tops the world record in the number of historic reconstructions – a feat both cheerful and sad, if you think how much must have been ruined to give rise to that exceptional effort of restoration.

The magic of objects that works in every city, regardless of the artistic and historical criteria, is a dominating factor in Warsaw. Nicolas Copernicus' monument in Krakowskie Przedmieście Street draws visitors' attention not only for being made by the great Danish sculptor, Bertel Thorvaldsen, but also for its unusual history over the last decades. In Poland's capital, every scrap of Gothic architecture and every porcellain collection are heroes of unusual tales of the lives of inanimate objects.

A word about Warsaw's Old Town.

A tiny section of today's city, it was for ages its major scene of events. Since the 16th century, crucial matters of urban and state importance were decided upon in the precinct of the Old Marketplace and within 300 metres from it. Warsaw's Old Town has been witness to major civilisational and social changes, but first of all, to the progress of history.

It has retained much of the atmosphere of the Vasa and Wettin dynasty, and even of the earlier Mazowsze Duchy times, bringing to the mind visions of crowds milling among the thicket of the market stalls, or watching public executions; or of the orderly ranks of French and Polish troops, ready for the commands of Napoleon

and Prince Józef Poniatowski, arriving up the steep Kamienne Schodki Street... And a hundred other episodes, mainly of martial nature.

The most recent of them, and still kept in living memory, is the Warsaw Uprising of 1944. Warsaw's Old Town area was then 90-percent ruined. Its narrow streets and small squares became the site of a raging battle, and the heroism of the ten thousand fighters, as well as the incredible suffering of Warsaw's citizens, will forever remain a haunting and glorious chart of Poland's history.

It is certainly worthwhile to visit Warsaw Old Town, where the Gothic meets the Baroque, and enter the Cathedral that had seen the crowning ceremonies of two Polish kings and the proclamation of the 3 May Constitution, as well as the wonderful, vivid local museum, offering ample food for historical thought.

But let us go beyond the old city walls. The King Zygmunt III Vasa Column that dominates Castle Square is one of the first (1644) secular monuments in Central Europe. Surrounded by waves of oncoming buses and cars, it soars over the underground tunnel, full of swishing twamways and automobiles. Now that the local traffic has been largely limited, the mildly sloping, awkwardly shaped terrace on which it stands, swarms with growing crowds of visitors.

Castle Square has had a dramatic and fascinating history. Its cobblestone area was many times strewn with dead bodies. The lofty King Zygmunt watched such terrible events as battles with the Swedes in 1656 and 1794, Kościuszko insurgents' fights with Russian and Prussian troops, or the 1944 uprising drama. Finally, the King himself tumbled down and shattered to pieces on the pavement.

When the clangor of the War died down, the King was returned to his lofty position. To his east, a new, airy construction of Śląsko-Dąbrowski Bridge was built, while the renovated "Royal Tract" ran toward him from the south. The neighbouring Krakowskie Przedmieście has sprung again with its palaces, churches and tenant houses, reconstructed thanks to the paintings by King Stanisław August Poniatowski's court artist Bernardo Belotto (known as Canaletto). The only local object that remained missing was the Royal Castle – for 200 years the seat of Polish monarchs and Parliament, and residence of the Republic's President between the Wars.

That last gap in the city-scape was filled at the end of the '70s. The quarter-century-plus break in the Castle's existence had been used for meticulous preparations of its reincarnation: the rescued substance was collected and put in order, and the satellite buildings of Pod Blachą Palace, Bacciarelli's House, Grodzka Gate, et al., were renovated. The Castle, built by eminent 16th–18th-century atchitects (Rodondo, Matthew Castelli, Giovanni Trevano, Jacob Fontana, Domenico Merlini, Johann Christian Kamsetzer, and others), is now back to its place in the Warsaw townscape.

Let us move back to the present.

Warsaw has several major traffic arteries. In the north-south direction, these include: the riverbank boulevards on both sides of the Vistula, the "Royal Tract," the chain of Andersa – Marszałkowska – Puławska streets, and the John Paul II Tract with Niepodległości Avenue. The major east-west transits are: Solidarność Avenue and Jerozolimskie Avenue with Washington Avenue. In 1974, another important, challenging and costly artery was completed, including a new bridge across the Vistula: it is Łazienkowska Tract.

If you are planning a longer stay in Warsaw, you may be advised to visit

Poland would not be possible without Krakow. At least, not the Poland we know, with its rich historical, cultural and intellectual background. National capital from the 11th to the late 16th century, the seat of the Polish kings, a treasury of arts and architecture, and one of the world's pioneer university centres (since the mid-14th century), Krakow has miraculously escaped the damage of the last War. Today, it is one of Europe's most precious historical cities.

A visitor to this spectacular urban phenomenon – the "Polish Athens" – is immediately plunged in the midst of a landscape remembering the times of the bow and arrow, the halberd and the battering-ram, with an atmosphere impossible to discover anywhere else in the modern world.

Parts of the Medieval Krakow city walls have survived, with Floriańska Gate (ca. 1300) and the Barbican (1498) – the latter presenting a rare type of European defence fortifications (a similar one can be seen in Carcassonne.)

Wawel Castle – parts of which are almost a thousand years old (the pre-Romanesque rotunda of St. Felix and St. Adauct was built in the 10th century!) – is ranked among the most imposing edifices of its kind in Europe. Looming over the city, the Castle epitomizes a vast portion of Krakow's history. Another epitome arrived only after World War II: it was the district of Nowa Huta [New Steelworks] – one of the major industrial enterprises in Communist Poland, with its own residential district of 200 thousand inhabitants. Nowa Huta was from the very start a political event: the idea was to saturate the royal city with a strong proletarian element. The social-engineering efforts proved futile. Alas, the smog from the steelworks has worked irreparable damage on Krakow's monuments of culture.

A growing modern university and cultural centre, Krakow still attracts people mainly with its historic heart. The original city, enclosed within the precinct of Planty park belt, has succumbed to the demands of modernity, accepting all its attributes, such as motor-vehicles, fashionable shops, neon lights and asphalt streets – and yet, it has not lost the stamp of the times past. The gargoyle-adorned façade of the Sukiennice [Cloth Market] building, occupying the centre of the Marketplace; Mariacki Church with the famous Wit Stwosz Altar and the bugle-call that resounds regularly from its tall tower; the 11th-century St. Andrew Church, the old Jagiellonian University campus, the narrow, bumpy, winding streets, the low gateways, the Medieval entrances and staircases, the many secret nooks and crannies – all are still there, for anyone to see and touch.

An important chapter of the city's cultural and social past falls to the district of Kazimierz – a separate township from the 14th century until 1791. Inhabited mainy be the Jewish population, it had been an important centre of Jewish religion and philosophy until World War II.

Krakow has always been home to the artistic and scientific elite, of Polish, as well as Italian, German and Czech origins. It was here that Jan Długosz wrote his *History of Poland* in the mid-15th century, here the star of Nicolas Copernicus was born. The city saw the life and work of the mathematician and astronomer Wojciech z Brudzewa, as well as of the great chemists, Zygmunt F. Wróblewski and Karol Olszewski. Krakow's famous painters were Jan Matejko and Stanisław Wyspiański. The list of local celebrities includes hundreds of names.

The ancient walls and monuments of culture are by no means the only

evidence of Krakow's past. Many old local customs have also been preserved – e.g. the parades opening the "green carnival," the production and exhibition of Christmas Nativity scenes, students' annual Juvenalia – the day when the Rector of the University confers his authority to the students who march across the city in a cheerful parade, dressed up as Medieval scholars. There is also *Lajkonik* – the "man-horse" – a tradition reaching back to the 13th century when the people of the suburban Półwieś Zwierzyniecki resisted a Tartar attack: each year, on the octave of Corpus Christi, during the "green carnival," a cheerful pageant of the Tartar Khan and his train starts across the city from St. Norbert Sisters' convent. Krakow has certainly had its good and bad times, of which *Lajkonik* is not the only proof. The royal city that had been a flourishing capital of Poland until the 17th century, went through a serious crisis a century later. In the 18th century, its 40-thousand population was reduced to 9 thousand. The streets and houses stood deserted. No sooner had the city recovered from that breakdown, than a new major disaster struck the entire country: following the Third Partition of Poland, Kraków became part of Austria, to gain the status of a free city for a brief 30 years, following the Vienna Congress. Back to the Austro-Hungarian administration, it was reduced to a provincial municipality – and yet, it never lost its importance as an academic and cultural centre, radiating intellectual refinement all over the triple-partitioned nation. It was in that, rather unfortunate, period that the strong ties between Krakow and Vienna were initiated, many Polish scientists (and some politicians) moving to the city on the Danube. Some of those old personal and cultural sentiments still prevail in Krakow, where the mildly sar-

castic jokes about Emperor Franz Joseph are still being told...

During the War, the magnificent Piast and Jagiellonian dynasties' residence of Wawel was usurped by Nazi governor Hans Frank, later executed under the charge of genocide, following the Nuremberg Trials. Among the Nazi victims were eminent professors of Jagiellonian University, arrested in the first days of the German occupation of the city.

More than a tousand years old, today's Krakow, with its population of 744 thousand, is not only the gem of Poland's national heritage, but also an important industrial, cultural and educational centre (with 15 academies and 12 seminaries.) It is the pride of every Polish citizen.

Recently renovated, it has become a delightful sister-town to Florence. People flock from all over the country to plunge into the cheerful crowd in the Market-place, diving into the hundreds of local bistros and cafés.

Wawel

In the hierarchy of Poland's national relics, the top place must be given to this craggy limestone hill, supporting a cluster of historical edifices, that looms over the Vistula River.

Its collection of art and archeology had grown for ten centuries. Between the 11th and the 16th centuries, Wawel Castle was the residence of Polish kings and queens. The two principal objects of Wawel are: the 13th–14th-century royal castle with its famous Renaissance arcaded courtyard and treasure-filled chambers, and the Romanesque-Gothic cathedral, hosting the tombs of the Polish monarchs and illustrious citizens.

The Wawel Hill harbours many a puzzling mystery. Between the 8th and the 10th centuries, it had supported a castle-town of the Wiślanie tribe. Fifty years ago, a pre-Romanesque

rotunda was discovered inside the present Castle walls, and, quite recently, new discoveries were reported – of the remnants of a 10th-century princely castle and of another pre-Romanesque rotunda. An unusual treasure of Wawel architecture is the golden-domed King Zygmunt Chapel (1517–1533) – a masterpiece by a Florentine architect and sculptor, Bartolomeo Berrecci.

Apart from the buildings and their interiors, the arcaded courtyard, too, deserves a special attention. It is ranked among the most beautiful and the oldest architectural objects of the kind, north of the Alps.

The Wawel tapestry collection shared the turbulent fates of many other Castle treasures. Made in Brussels, in the mid-16th century, on the order of King Zygmunt August II, the tapestries had been repeatedly stolen, shipped away and damaged – until, in 1961, they made their final come-back to Wawel Castle, following a chain of eventful War-time peregrinations.

The Castle also contains wonderfully preserved Persian and Turkish tents of the 17th and the 18th centuries.

An object of general admiration is the Envoy Chamber, with its 16th-century carved coffer ceiling, featuring human heads.

Regalia of great value (including St. Maurice's Spear) and cult objects that had been collected since the Middle Ages, are locked in the Crown Treasury – part of the National Art Collection of Wawel, and in the Cathedral Treasury, while precious manuscripts remain in the custody of the Chapter Library.

During the Nazi occupation, Wawel Castle was seriously damaged – some historic chambers were modernized, the royal stables were demolished – and many items of its arms, arts and craft collections (e.g. the golden goblet of King Zygmunt II Vasa that has never been returned from Germany) were shipped away.

Wawel Castle is probably the greatest tourist attraction in Poland. Each year, the Wawel Hill is visited by some 2 million tourists.

On important national occasions, the famous Zygumnt Bell (of 1520) is rung: sonorous and huge, it measures 8 metres in circumference.

The younger generations have traditionally been much impressed by the legend of the Wawel Dragon, reported to have made its lair at the foot of the Castle Hill, in a den overlooking the Vistula, and indulge in the nasty habit of consuming people (especially young maidens) – until it was cunningly assassinated by a brave young cobbler.

Silesia

Some geographical names instantly bring to the mind visions of smoking factory chimneys, coal mounds, loaded trucks and men in crash helmets: this is true of the French Nord, the German Ruhra, the British Manchester – sprawling industrial complexes with no beginning and no end.

Another one is the Polish Silesia [Śląsk]. An area to the south-west of the country, it abounds in natural treasures that have been stubbornly excavated from its bowels for the last hundreds of years.

Coal and steel production – the two staples of the local industry – have been losing importance against new, powerful branches of electronic, motor, food and other industries. The giant coal-mines and steelworks of this one-time privileged economic zone, are being accused of destroying the environment. Deep structural transformations in Silesia give rise to a growing social unrest – a phenomenon also familiar in many other European countries.

The proverbially "black" Silesia has its green side, too, with a strong

tourist base including fashionable resort centres of Jaszowiec and Wisła. It also has its forests, meadows and gardens – a plethora of colourfully overgrown "lilliputian" cultivation plots.

In the very midst of the Upper-Silesia Industrial District, between the cities of Katowice and Chorzów, an immense public park has been planted on the wasteland of former excavation grounds. One of the largest in Europe, the Park of Culture and Recreation offers swimming-pools, playgrounds, exhibition halls, a 90-thousand-seat stadium, restaurants, hectares of garden, and even a planetarium. Though imposing, it cannot alter the sad truth about Silesia's dramatic ecological condition.

Many coal-mines and steelworks are now operated by computers (made abroad, or in the neighbouring Upper Silesia,) but many others are working relics of the mining methods of centuries ago. Special events of the local history are also cherished and proudly recalled – e.g. the farewell *rendez-vous*, in Tarnowskie Góry, of King Jan Sobieski and his beloved wife, Queen Mary (lovingly nicknamed "Marysieńka"), on the eve of the royal campaign to aid the besieged Vienna – another bright accent in the not so very black picture of Silesia.

Gdańsk

A frequent bone of contention throughout the 20 years that separated the two World Wars, the Free City of Gdańsk became Hitler's demagogic argument for invading Poland. The canonnade that started World War II was opened in the early hours of 1 September, 1939, by the battleship "Schleswig-Holstein" aiming at Polish guard posts on Cape Westerplatte.

Another milestone of global history that is inseparably connected with Gdańsk, was the birth of "Solidar-ność," in August, 1980, following a major strike at the Gdańsk Shipyard and igniting a fierce social protest that soon swept over the whole country.

The oldest historical record of Gdańsk comes from the first millenium, and is dated A.D. 999 (in *The Life of St. Adalbert.*) Since then, the busy urban port and trade centre has been frequently mentioned in many documents. In 1308, the city was cunningly conquered by the Teutonic Knights, who largely destroyed it, murdering the inhabitants. For nearly 150 following years, Gdańsk was the seat of the Teutonic Knights Order. Returned to Poland in 1466, it remained a Polish city until the end of the First Republic. Thanks to a number of royal privileges that the city enjoyed, as well as its monopoly on overseas corn and timber trade, Gdańsk became widely famous for its wonderful architecture and lavish works of art.

Much of its long-hoarded wealth perished in the last War. The city's reconstruction was painstaking, but worth the effort. Within the precinct of the so-called Main City, we may now admire a great number of restored historic objects: Długi Targ [Long Market Lane,] the Armoury, Wyżynna [Highway] Gate, the Executioner's House, the Prison Tower, the Golden Gate, St. George Fraternity Court, St. Mary's Church, the Royal Chapel, the Artus' Court, the Town-hall, etc.

Gdańsk is part of the urban triplet of Gdańsk-Sopot-Gdynia. An important industrial centre and a busy sea-port, it is also the seat of six academies and many important cultural institutions. Besides its history and monuments, Gdańsk is also famous for the manufacturing of stylish furniture and an original brand of vodka ("Goldwasser") – as well as for harbouring the private residence of Lech Wałęsa.

Situated in the Gdańsk Bay, this beautiful, old city deserves a tourist's attention. Having visited the Main Town-hall, the Old Town, the Old Suburbs, the Lower City and the cornhouses on the Motława, visitors are advised to proceed to the Monument to the Shipyard Victims (the three towering crosses) and the Monument to the Heroes of Westerplatte. They may also pay homage to the defenders of Gdańsk Post-Office, listen to an organ concert at Oliwa Cathedral, and take a walk along the longest (512 metres) Polish pier in Sopot.

Kielce

Some say that Poland started here, in Kielce – the true national cradle (but beware: the same has been said of Poznań and Kraków.)

Kielce is an urban centre of 200-thousand-plus inhabitants, spread over picuresquely forrested hills. Its name was first recorded in the 11th-century chronicles. Its two prize historical monuments are: the Baroque-style Krakovian Bishops' Palace, now housing Kielce National Museum, and the 17th-century early-Baroque Cathedral. The Palace, built between 1637 and 1641 by Thomas Poncino and other masters, boasts wonderful interiors, full of stucco and polychrome ornaments and topped with painted ceilings (done by artists from Thomas Dolabella's workshop.) The Renaissance tomb inside the Cathedral is attributed to Giovanni Maria Padovano. Traditionally a town of narrow streets, Kielce is being teansformed into a modern urban centre, with new, wide arteries and glass towers of the office buildings. It is losing its habitual status of a "lovable backwater," to become a swinging metropolis. But the local treasures of the past have not been neglected. Neither have the dramatic events of the local history: the days of the Nazi occupation, when Kielce was a major centre of partisan and conspiracy organisations, or the Jewish *pogrom* (lynch) of 1946, whose circumstances and political background still await full explanation.

Having found accommodation in Kielce, you may venture on many shorter and longer local trips: eastwards, to Szydłowa – one of the few Polish towns with original old fortifications; or to Nietulisko, to visit the ruins of an ancient dam. You may also visit the antique town of Opatów; or go to Krzyżtopór Castle in the neighbourhood of Ujazd – a one-time rival of the Royal Wawel Castle in Krakow. In Klimontów village you will see a Baroque Collegiate Church. We also recommend visiting Pińczów – once an important centre of the Polish Reformation.

Kilece cultivates noble cultural traditions. It used to be the centre of activity of the illustrious Polish citizen, Stanisław Staszic. In 1958, Kielce Scientific Society was founded, to explore the Świętokrzyski Region – an exceptionally vast and rewarding field of research.

Wrocław

In 1948, Pablo Picasso saw the dynamic reconstruction of Wrocław as a stimulus to the local artistic activity. To Ilya Erenburg, Wrocław appeared a typically Polish city – not just for its ancient walls that remembered the times of King Bolesław Krzywousty, but, rather, for the thousands of Polish pioneers, breathing new life into the old, dead walls. Neither Picasso, nor Eernburg, mentioned the new Wrocław settlers: Polish citizens exiled from the areas across the River Bug, mainly from the city of Lvov.

Poland's third most populated city, after Warsaw and Łódź, today's Wrocław is home to 850 thousand inhabitants. It has dozens of industries, the major

ones being: the railway coach factory of Pafawag, and the two electronic equipment producers – Elwro and Dolmel. The city's style is dictated by its eight academies. And a number of internationally famous artistic centres attract crowds of professionals and amateurs. Wrocław was the cradle of Henryk Tomaszewski's Pantomime Theatre, and Jerzy Grotowski's Laboratorium Theatre. It is Poland's second (to Warsaw) theatre centre. To complete the city's cultural picture, let us mention the venerable Ossolineum Institute with its vast book collection, the museums, the Film Company (producer of Andrzej Wajda's *Ashes and Diamond*,) and a multitude of locally held national and international culture festivals. A special tourist attraction is the painting called *Panorama Racławicka*, exhibited in a specially built rotunda – a huge canvas by a group of painters, with Wojciech Kossak and Jan Styka.

Wrocław's central historical spot is Ostrów Tumski. Restored from serious War-time damage, it includes the 13th–14th-century Cathedral Church, with the magnificent Marian, St. Elizabeth's and Electoral chapels, as well as the Holy Cross Church, of the same period.

Outside Ostrów Tumski lies the historical complex of Piasek, the old Market-place with its late-Gothic Townhall, churches and tenements (one of them, a twin building with an arcaded link, situated on the north-western side of the Market-place, is known as Hansel and Gretel, courtesy Grimm brothers.)

Gothic and Baroque masters never grudged Wrocław their talents. Alas, in 1945, the Nazi proclaimed Wrocław their stronghold, thus signing the city's death sentence: it was 70-percent ruined at the end of the War.

Let us conclude with a brief historical summary: Wrocław had originally belonged to the Polish Piast dynasty;

in 1335 it was occupied by the Czech; in 1526 – by the Habsburgs; in 1741 – by the Prussians. Yet, it was always – even during the long period of Germanization – economically and culturally connected with Poland.

Poznań

Contrary to the belief of some people in the wide world, Poznań is not just the International Poznań Fair – though the great annual commercial carnival is of a major local and national importance. Poznań's trading traditions go back to the Middle Ages.

It all started back in 1231, when Duke Władysław Odonic lifted the taxes off all the merchandise brought into the city on the octave of St. Dominic's day. In 1394, a new and even more effective reform was introduced, called the "privilege of storing." The "privilege" that was, in fact, a duty, soon proved its benefits. All foreign traders who crossed Poznań on their journey along the amber trail, were obliged to hold their merchandise on display for three days. By the mid-15th century, the local "St. John Fairs" became an official institution that soon won recognition all over Europe, as well as in the Near and Far East.

In 1925, its modern counterpart – Poznań International Fair – was initiated.

In 1994, the six-day Fair, traditionally held in June, brought 127 million

Poznań, the interior of the Town-hall

The Town-hall in Toruń

zloty. Poznań's staple commercial event, it has been getting more and more competition from specialist motor, tourist and – especially – Polagra fairs.

Poznań is one of Poland's biggest and oldest cities. Situated at the crossing of major transport routes, it boasts eight academies, a number of important cultural institutions (with the famous Opera,) several big industrial companies (e.g. "Cegielski" ship-engine and railway-carriage producers, or electronic, rubber, paper and food factories,)

As early as the mid-10th century, a princely castle-town stood in the delta between the Warta and the Cybina rivers. At the turn of the 11th century, Poznań became Poland's capital. A bishopric since 968, it acquired foundation charters in 1253. From then on, local trade prospered better and better. In 1519, Lubrański Science Academy was founded in Poznań, as a branch of Krakow Academy. The city's later history abounds in sad events: the Swedish Wars, natural disasters, struggles with Germanization, Wielkopolskie [Greater-Polish] Uprising against the Germans, the trauma of the Nazi occupation, and the cruel battles of 1945 that resulted in a serious destruction of the city.

In 1956, the streets of Poznań became the scene of a brutally quenched social protest – the first post-War mass mutiny of the workers.

What has been left of the city 's turbulent past? The list is quite long. It is enough to visit the historic Old Town with the Old Market-place, surrounded by 15th–17th-century houses (reconstructed after the War), the Działyński Palace – the seat of several of scientific institutes, Odwach (1787) and the building of the old Weights House (demolished in 1890 and reconstructed in 1960.) Close by, stands the Military Museum and the

charming, Empire-style Mielżyński Palace.

Poznań's major historical building is the Town-hall. Built in the 13th century (the original early-Gothic basement has survived), it was expanded in 1550–1560 in Renaissance style, by Giovanni Battista Quadro. Partly ruined in 1945, it has been carefully reconstructed. Its eastern facade, with a circular arcade and an open loggia, is especially impressive. On the first floor is the imposing Renaissance Hall – one of the most valuable Renaissance interiors north of the Alps. The Town-hall harbours the History Museum.

Poznań's Old Town abounds in objects of interest: there is Poland's unique Museum of Musical Instruments in the Old Market-place, the parish church that is one of Poland's most beautiful Baroque sanctuaries, the National Museum at the foot of Przemysław's Hill, the Cathedral whose fragments date back to the 10th century, and a number of interesting churches.

As everybody in Poznań knows, advertising is the engine of art.

Toruń

Ask a Polish child what he or she knows about Toruń, and you will hear: Copernicus and ginger-bread. Those better educated in the national tourist attractions may add the Leaning

Toruń, the Palace of Kujavian Bishops

Szczecin, the Castle of the Pomeranian Princes

Tower, the Town-hall in the Old Market-place, and, perhaps, the seven-ton "God's Trumpet" in St. John's church – Poland's second biggest bell (the first being Krakow's "Zygmunt".)

Toruń is one of the most popular Polish towns. Its interesting Old Town complex includes several especially noteworthy objects: the 15th-century Town-hall and its 13th-century tower, built by Master Andrzej and rebuilt, in mannerist style, by Anthony van Obbergen; Gothic churches of St. John (c. 14), Our Lady (c. 13) and St. James (c. 14); a number of gates and keeps, with the famous 14th-century leaning tower whose top leans 1.40m off the perpendicular; the old New Market tenements and inns, and many others.

The local authorities of Toruń have been more daring than their counterparts in other Polish cities in creating experimental combinations of traditional and modern architecture (e.g. on the Vistula escarpment.) Among the Castle ruins, *son et lumière* shows are organised.

Crucial facts from Toruń's history include: getting the municipal rights in 1233, becoming of a major anti-Tutonic resistance centre during the 13-Years' War, going back to the Polish administration in 1466, supporting of Polish Protestant movement during the Reformation.

Still, the most important date in the local history is 19 February, 1473 – the birthday of one of humanity's greatest minds, Nicolas Copernicus, son of a wealthy merchant.

Despite its considerable post-War expansion (in 1991, Toruń's population topped 200 thousand), the youthful expansion of the local university – named, of course, after Nicolas Copernicus, and the modern production plants – the narrow streets and Gothic walls have preserved much of the atmosphere of the times when Copernicus worked here on his heliocentric theory of the Universe.

And remember to try the delicious gingerbread – made by the "Kopernik" Company.

Szczecin

A sprawling city – Poland's third in area (284km^2), following Warsaw and Wrocław – Szczecin is the country's biggest sea port, as well as an important industrial and cultural centre.

Inhabited by more than 400 thousand citizens, it abounds in green areas and bold town-planning solutions, modelled on those of Paris.

At the end of the 10th century, Szczecin became part of Poland. In 1124, the native population of the "900 family fathers" recorded in the annals were christened by the Poles. The area has been raided by the Danes, the Swedes, the Prussians, and even the French. The Szczecin that was returned to Poland after World War II was half-ruin, its port and industrial substance 95-percent destroyed. The city thus began its second millenium from scratch – to achieve a widely-acclaimed success.

In August 1980, Szczecin became, like Gdańsk, a scene of mass workers' strikes and a bastion of "Solidarność." Let us look around for the city's past preserved in stone. There is, of course, the Castle of the Pomeranian Princes: alternately destroyed and reconstructed, it makes a meaningful document of the area's erratic history. There are the Gothic churches of St. James (c. 14–15) and of St. Peter and Paul (c. 15). There is the Town-hall (c. 13–14), the Loitz House (c. 16), and the two city gates: Port Gate and Prussian Tribute Gate.

Nowadays, Szczecin is a busy metropolis, teeming with sailors, youngsters and tourists from Germany and Scandinavia.

Spectacularly situated, it lies on the Oder River – flanked by the double-tier Chrobry Dyke that encourages long promenades – and is partly immersed in the sprawling, dense forests: two major landscape assets beyond competition.

In fact, the entire neighbourhood abounds in forests, waters and Gothic constructions.

Płock

Few people know that Płock was once shortlisted to become the national capital, and it was only by some unexplained decree of fate that the honour eventually befell Warsaw.

The map of Poland confirms the attractive situation of the city that is both Poland's major petrochemical industry centre (intersected by the Russian pipeline.) and a valued historical complex.

Płock is one of Poland's oldest towns. The first records of its existence come from the second half of the 10th century. For some time, since the 11th century, Płock had functioned as a temporary capital of Mazowsze and a royal residence – it is still a seat of the bishopric. It has always been an important political and cultural centre.

Spectacularly situated on a lofty bank of the Vistula, Płock is especially famous for its castle-cathedral complex on Tumskie Hill (whose slopes reveal a worrying tendency to slide.) The only remnants of the ruined castle are: the Clock Tower (c. 13th–14th) and the Gentry Tower. Nearby stands an old Benedictine abbey, with a lovely courtyard. There are 18th–19th-century corn-houses by the river, and the Old Town boasts a Classicist Town-hall, built in 1826. But the city's prize treasure is the Romanesque Cathedral (its original 12th-century features have changed beyond recognition as a result of many renovations), with the sar-cophagi of kings Wadysław Herman and Bolesław Krzywousty.

Just like Krakow with its Nowa Huta, Płock is a typical example of the coexistence of two different epochs and civilizations. The coupling creates an interesting, dynamic effect, that is not entirely harmonious.

Zakopane and the Tatra Mountains

Zakopane is a resort town cradled at the foot of the Tatra range. The winter capital of Poland, it lies at the altitude of 900 metres above sea level. Its merits were discovered some one hundred years ago by a famous local animator, Dr Tytus Chałubiński. Soon, the modest village of Zakopane was transformed into a mecca for writers, composers and painters. Some time later, the sportsmen arrived. The local style in architecture, furniture and decoration was refined and carefully cultivated. Zakopane became a reputed leisure and resort centre – though in the later years its environment suffered considerably from smog.

The town has its local Tatra Museum in the principal promenade of Krupówki, as well as a lovely wooden church of 1847, with the cemetery where many great artists have been buried – among them "the Homer of the Tatras," Jan Sabała Krzeptowski, the famous storyteller and author of many local folk songs. Jan Kasprowicz – a great Polish poet and admirer of Podhale Region – has his monographic museum in nearby Harenda.

Although the architecture of modern Zakopane has been an object of fervent dispute in which the tourist agencies are much criticised, nobody can deny that the area has a unique magnetism that attracts crowds of admirers.

Zakopane is the main base for Tatra climbers. Much lower than the Alps, with the highest peak – the Slovakian Gerlach – at a mere 2663m, the Tatras

are, nevertheless, known as wild, rough and demanding mountains. Erosion of the rocks, caused by the ice and the permanent snow, results in the formation of cliffs, crags and sharp ridges. The rocky basins have become lakes (43 are on the Polish side of the Tatras,) spurting waterfalls down from high terraces. The Tatran flora includes 1700 plant species, some of them relics from the tertiary era. In spring, Tatra meadows and sprawling valleys are overgrown, carpet-like, with crocuses. As for the local fauna, you may meet a brown bear (beware!), a lynx, a badger, a marmot, a chamois, an eagle, or a salamander.

Periodical warm Tatra winds, the so-called *halny*, can be quite violent, uprooting trees, tearing roofs off the buildings, and, sometimes, knocking down vast areas of woods. When *halny* blows, many people up in the mountains and down in the valleys complain of nervous tensions and palpitations. For thousands of years, the Tatra valleys at the foot of this 57-kilometre-long and 18-kilometre-wide mountain range, had been an area of continuous migrations. Local sheep-grazing has preserved its traditional forms, originating from the Balkan-Rumanian shepherding culture. A fascinating chapter of the local past is the Tatra treasure hunt that preceded modern coal-mining. Certain amounts of gold and copper ores had been excavated in the region of Mount Krywań since the 16th century, while coal-mines and smelteries were started later, especially in Kościeliska Valley.

The breathtaking Tatra landscapes have been immortalized in poems and symphonies, as well as, more recently, on colour postcards, featuring Lake Marine Eye (is not the very name sheer poetry?), the Black Lake, Chochołowska, Strażyska, Gasienicowa and Kondratowa Valleys, Mount Rysy, Mount Giewont, Mount Red Peaks, or Roztoka Valley. Still, visitors from the city prefer to take a comfortable cable-car ride to the top of Mount Kasprowy, or Mount Gubałówka, which provide the real, exceptional mountain views. During the tourist season (from January to March and from June to September,) Zakopane is raided by hordes of enthusiasts. Not all of them are capable of experiencing the mountains as deeply as writers Stanisław Ignacy Witkiewicz-„Witkacy," Kazimierz Tetmajer and Jan Kasprowicz, or composers Mieczysław Karłowicz and Karol Szymanowski. But they will be excused, as long as they observe the regulations of the Tatra National Park – "do not pick plants, do not damage the area, do not dump rubbish" – and mind the safety rules. Should they ignore the latter, the Mountain Volunteer Rescue Team [GOPR] – an organisation with half-a-century tradition – is there to help.

Zakopane has aspired – so far, in vain – to hosting the Winter Olympic Games, the idea gaining as many advocates, as it had opponents.

A popular foreign-published tourist guide declares: "There are many regions and towns in Poland you may miss, but you must not, on any account, miss the Tatras and Zakopane." The latter part of the statement is beyond dispute.

Błędowska Desert

Stretching not far from Olkusz is the only desert in Central Europe. Its area of moving sands is about 32 square kilometres (8 x 4km.) with 2.3 billion cubic metres of sand, forming dunes, some of which are umpteen-metres high. Sadly, the Polish Sahara has been shrinking, due to continued industrial exploitation of its western part.

Crossing Błędowska Desert is the River Biała Przemsza, its banks overgrown with lavish greenery, to resemble an elongated oasis. The dunes grow clusters of sharp-edged grass. Gales and sand-storms sometimes sweep over the area, and the phenomenon of mirages is, reportedly, no great rarity in the summer.

The desert is surrounded by pine woods. The view from the church-tower in Błędowo may well compete with those you get from a minaret in Tunisia. To the west, Błędowska Desert borders on the Green Lake, reportedly, the site of a one-time silver mine.

Many Stone Age objects have been discovered by archaeologists in the desert. Sand is known to be an excellent preservative.

During the Nazi occupation, Marshall Rommel made the sandy Olkusz area training grounds for his troops. It is from Błędowska Desert that the German troops were transported to North Africa. Nowadays, the miniature desert is often used by low-budget film producers.

Błędowska Desert is an exceptional curiosity, offering a few hours of welcome relaxation to those exhausted by the sight-seeing of Krakow, Ojców, Pieskowa Skała and other local wonders. Children may occupy themselves by building sand castles, while the grown-ups will enjoy the charms of the mirage. But you must make haste: in fifteen years' time, the desert may not be there any longer.

The Pieniny Mountains

They are – even more than the Tatras – mountains within mountains: an exceptionally beautiful cluster of limestone hills, set amongst the long Carpathian range. The 9-kilometre stretch of the Dunajec River, picturesquely meandering between the towering rocks, can be sailed on rafts, made up of hollowed tree-trunks tied together: tourists then become spectators to a powerful drama performed by Nature and Element. The entertainment is as safe, as it is exciting.

Two symbolic wardens of the Pieniny are the castles of Czorsztyn and Niedzica. The former – built in the 14th century for the famous knight Zawisza Czarny – became the stronghold of a 17th-century peasant revolt; burnt down, it has survived only as a ruin. The castle in Niedzica has been partly reconstructed and its Renaissance wing is now used by the art historians as a hotel-workshop unit.

The Pieniny National Park, established several decades ago, harbours more than a thousand species of plants and is overgrown with firs, beeches, yews and larches. Its meadows are full of flowers. Some of the plants growing in the rocky cracks are tertiary specimens.

This peaceful world of natural beauty is being more and more aggressively attacked by modern civilization, especially in its motorized version. The dam across the Dunajec, that was for years an object of fierce ecological protests, has now become a fact – causing no major disaster.

The Pieniny Mountains occupy a mere 2708 hectares, but the density of the local beauty and uniqueness is exceptionally high.

Stary Sącz

Old [stary] it is indeed, the town in Sądecka Valley, on the Poprad River.

close to the mouth of the Dunajec. It had been mentioned as a castle-town as early as 1224, soon to acquire municipal rights (1273) and its first tax privileges, decreed by King Bolesław Wstydliwy.

Stary is a popular adjunct to Polish settlement names, to quote only Stary Gostyń, Stary Targ, Stary Wiśnicz, or Stary Zamość. All those, however, have village status. Stary Sącz is the only urban exception to the rule – though its size and population (of 8.6 thousand) are far from imposing. It is a township, rather than a town, that cannot compare with the neighbouring Nowy [New] Sącz – city of 80,000 that has only recently lost its rank of the voivodship capital. Surprisingly, Nowy Sącz is not so very new, either, being a mere 50 years younger than its senior by the same name.

The irresistible beauty of Stary Sącz brings to the mind the miniature towns of Italy and southern France. Its Medieval street arrangement has been left intact by the War and modern architects' fantasies – which borders on a miracle, considering that during the last War Stary Sącz was an important partisan base (its population reduced to 1.5 thousand,) and after the War, there have been many plans to "modernize" its architecture. Stary Sącz is a historical town, with the buildings of St. Clare Sisters' Convent, founded in 1280 by the recently canonized St. Kinga, and the Gothic Holy Trinity Church of 1332. Even in the Market-place – though its surrounding tenements are younger, belonging to the Baroque – the breath of antiquity is strongly felt: the modestly-proportioned Market-place is truly moving in its provincialism, far from imitating the splendour of Kraków or Toruń. The striking modesty of the town's architecture may have been the result of the local guild traditions: the cobblers and potters who inhabited Stary Sącz were hardly the people to afford lavish residential homes.

But they paid much attention to order and cleanliness, and favoured the construction of public buildings – especially churches. Holy Trinity Church has been for centuries the pride of the town. It has survived all kinds of cataclysms, including the great fire, set in 1410 by the Hungarian King Sigmund Luxemburg. The church has a 16th-century vaulted nave, a Baroque pulpit, stucco altars (built in 1669 by Baltazar Fontana,) a Gothic chapel of St. Kinga, a collection of paintings and sculptures (some also Gothic,) a treasury, and the adjoining monastery building with the cloister (by J. de Simon, 1605) covered in sgraffito. Indeed, it is a sanctuary one would rather expect in a metropolis.

Stary Sącz is the pearl of the Sadecka province, a lovely area surrounding the Poprad and the Dunajec rivers and bordering on the Beskidy mountain ranges of Jaworzyna and Radziejowa. The region abounds in townships, spas, and villages that seem to have been taken out of 19th-century sketchbooks. There are the local hills for climbers and skiers, the rivers for canoers and anglers, the fruit orchards and apiaries for gourmets; and the locally-produced liquors – for all.

The Bieszczady

Not so long ago, an overworked or depressed Pole might have said: "I'll get me down to the Bieszczady and bury myself in the bush." Well, burying oneself in the bush is not so easy nowadays, as the part of the Beskid Mountains called the Bieszczady is no longer a Polish Siberia or Amazonia. Civilization invades with a growing impetus. Perhaps it is for the better – but still, it leaves one sad. Nevertheless, the area between the Łupkowska Pass and the River Solina to the west,

and the Świeca River to the east, continues to be the least populated part of Poland; it is also industry-free and densely forrested. The broad, sun-flooded meadows among the woods are grazing grounds for the local sheep, only occasionally troubled by a hungry predator (which may happen to be a brown bear.)

The entire Bieszczady is an area of a mere 120 by 90 kilometres, with the highest peaks of Tarnica (1346m), Krzemień (1335m) and Halicz (1333m). Winding through the mountains is one of Poland's most picturesque motorways, called Pętla Bieszczadzka [Bieszczady Loop]. A popular tourist centre is Solina, on the vast reservoir that was created following the construction of a dam on the San. Another local recreation spot is the luxury complex of Arłamowo – once reserved for the Communist establishment (who, during Martial Law, used it to intern Lech Wałęsa,) it is now opened for the general public.

In the immediately post-War years, the Bieszczady became the scene of a bloody Polish-Ukrainian conflict, followed by mass deportations (the so-called "Wisła Project") of the Ukrainian population. The shameful action banished many local families, and even entire villages, to other parts of the country.

The Bieszczady Region abounds in charming nooks and crannies, countless wooden Orthodox churches, trout-filled rivers, and deep forests inhabited by bisons (more than a dozen, out of Poland's 60!), lynxes, wildcats, deer and wolves, while the fruitful underbrush offers berries, wild mushrooms and hazelnuts. The few local towns and villages are centuries old – to name only 14th-century Lesko, with a 16th-century Jewish cemetery and a synagogue (now made a museum.)

Nine kilometres to the north-east of Ustrzyki Dolne, in Krościenko, on the Polish-Ukrainian border, live some of the Greek families who sought refuge in Poland in 1949, following the Greek civil war – the rest have returned home. The Bieszczady is a watershed dividing the catchment areas of the Baltic Sea and the Black Sea.

Thriller fans will be glad to know that, in some thickets off the main tourist routes, they may face not only a brown bear and a wolf, but also a poisonous snake.

Among the sprawling valleys and breath-taking river gorges, amidst the fir, beech, yew and sycamore woods, a visitor may take a deep breath of reviving, clean air, before his is plunged back in the midst of the stiffling vapours of civilization.

The Augustowski Canal

In 1824, the authorities of the Congress Kingdom decided to build a waterway that would connect the Vistula basin, across the Niemen, with the Kurland Baltic ports. The idea behind the project was to save Polish and Lithuanian trade companies the troublesome necessity of using Prussian transit routes. (Prussia had cut off the Polish Congress Kingdom from the sea and controlled its economic relations with the West.) The construction of the Augustowski Canal – a new waterway running through the territory of the Polish Congress Kingdom – was completed within 12 years, to the amazement and admiration of all Europe. The constructors were officers of the Engineering Corps, commanded by Ignacy Prądzyński.

The Augustowski Canal is now a unique example of traditional engineering in Poland, few similar objects matching it in Europe. It is still navigable, even for 100-ton ships. The Canal's uniqueness finds a perfect match in the beauty of the surrounding landscape. The waterway is naturally continued by the Czarna Hańcza, a tributary of the

Niemen – a paradise for canoers and anglers. In Augustów – the town of 3,000 – there are some original Canal buildings and installations.

Presently, only an 80 kilometre stretch of the 102-kilometre-long Canal is on the Polish territory, with 14 (out of 18) original canal locks. The Canal connects a number of lovely local lakes: Lake Necko, Lake Białe, Lake Augustowskie and Lake Studzienniczne. Amazingly, the old mechanisms opening and closing the locks are still in working condition. A stunning relic, Augustowski Canal is, indeed, something like a Bugatti automobile, or a Wright Brothers' aeroplane. As it cannot be transported to a museum, you have to admire it on the site.

The Oak Trees of Rogalin

Trees can also become historical monuments – provided they survive several hundred years. If they do, they become monuments to man's blessed negligence that saved them from the axe.

In Rogalin on the Warta River (33 kilometres from Poznań), beside the Baroque-Classicist palace, built 1770–1782 and filled with period furniture and paintings, there is a historic park, with Europe's biggest cluster of old oak trees.

There are 954 oak trees growing in Rogalin. Three of them – bearing the names of the legendary Slav brothers: Lech, Czech and Rus – are 9, 7.30 and 6.70 metres in circumference. They serve as the background for group photographs of visiting school-children, who stand around the tree-trunks, holding hands.

The Rogalin oak-trees have been pestered by longicorns – an insect species that is quite unusual in Poland. The war between the longicorn and the ecologists continues.

Let us remind the readers that in pre-Christian times, the oak was revered as a sacred tree in many parts of Europe (e.g. in Lithuania.) Its name is quoted in many ancient folk chants and proverbs. Oak timber is heavy and hard, its bark rich in tannine.

The village of Rogalin was reportedly first mentioned in the chronicles of the year 1247. However, only the local oak trees may now confirm the information.

Świętokrzyskie Mountains

This sandstone-and-quartz mountain range of a modest height (up to 612 metres) lies in the very heart of Poland. It is densely overgrown with fir forests, and on Mount Chełmowa there are wonderful larch woods.

The most beautiful section of the range is the National Park (6046 hectares), dedicated to the writer Stefan Żeromski – the great bard of the region. A special local attraction is the Holy Cross monastery complex on top of Łysa Góra [Bald Mountain,] founded in the 12th century and successively expanded, used as one of the hardest Polish prisons until the last War.

Some locals still wear traditional folk costumes. The region saw the birth of the Polish iron-ore mining and smelting – a tradition that is annually celebrated with "Dymarki" [Smelting Festival.] The area also offers excellent sandstone.

The Świętokrzyskie Mountains have a rich tradition of warfare: during the

last War, they were controlled by strong partisan troops. Between October 1939 and late April 1940, the brave Major Henryk Dobrzański – "Hubal," later immortalized in a number of books and a film – commanded his troops in the region.

The mountains and their neighbourhood are dotted with priceless, authentic relics of the past, embedded in the natural country landscape. The surroundings offer some truly exotic flora. In the steppe reservation of Chotl Czerwony, the phenomenon of "burning Moses bushes" has been observed: the locally growing Asian species of dittany shrubs produce spontaneously combustible volatile oils that burn with red and blue flames. Also in Chotl, you may see giant gypsum crystals, some of them 2m high – a phenomenon that is unique in the world.

A few kilometres south of the main range, there is a cluster of smaller hills, supporting the castle-town (or, rather, its 13th-century ruin) of Chęciny. Some years ago, it served as the setting of *Master Wołodyjowski* – a film based on the novel by Henyk Sienkiewicz: one of the castle towers was then renovated. The nearby reservation with Raj [Paradise] Cave is open for tourists.

The Sundials at Jędrzejów

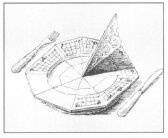

A town situated on the busy Warsaw-Krakow route, Jędrzejów boasts a history of more than 700 years. But its antiquity is not the only reason for its fame. Neither is the local Cistercian

church and monastery, built in the 12th century and rebuilt in Baroque style in the 1730s. Nor the fact that it was in Jędrzejów that Wincenty Kadłubek (1150–1223) wrote his famous Polish chronicles.

The Market-place of Jędrzejów is the address of one of the three major sundial museums in the world. Founded by Feliks Przypkowski, it was later managed by his son, the late Tadeusz Przypkowski, PhD – one of the two world-famous active gnomonists. Przypkowski would sometimes go abroad to build a sundial in Spain, or in Greece – but most of his days were spent in Jędrzejów museum, among its 500 rare exhibits.

Some of the displayed items are centuries old, but there are also some army sudials from the last War, including the so-called gnomonic slider which the Nazis had used during the bombardment of Warsaw, in 1939. Jędrzejów is worth visiting. The museum presently receives several hundred spectators a day. You may well set your watch according to the Jędrzejów gnomon, as it perfectly indicates the azimuth of the Sun.

Tourists are also intrigued by a small dome that dominates the roofs of the Marketplace tenements. It tops the observatory – another passion of the learned man, Przypkowski – to name only the main areas of his multifarious activity – was also an excellent gastronomer, gourmet and chef. He had planned to set up a restaurant in Jędrzejów, serving local specialities, such as "Przypkowski Soup" and "Pork Loin Jędrzejów Style." The museum has a special kitchen section, with 17th–19th-century pots and utensils, old (18th–19th-century) prints and manuscripts on gastronomy, as well as culinary libraries, including one that used to belong to Pomian Pożerski in Paris.

Next door to the museum is a phar-

macy, established in 1712 by the Patek family. Their heir, Anthony, set up the famous watch factory in Geneva that prospers to this day, known as the "Patek Philippe" Company.

Białowieska Forest

In the river basin of the Narew and the Jasiolda, in Poland's eastern borderland, spreads the largest Central-European forest – witness to the thousand-years' history of the local people. Hard as their lives must have been a millenium ago, threatened by the wilderness, the marshes and a multitude of savage predators – we, citizens of the world of motorways, electricity, television and refrigerators, cannot help feeling an occasional pang of nostalgy for the irrevocable past. But Białowieska Forest still contains some of it – despite the elegant hotel in Białowieża, the smooth motorway and the neon sign over a local shop.

The entire forest occupies the area of 1250km^2, 580km^2 spreading over the Polish territory. Part of it (5069ha) is Białowieski National Park, with the 4700-hectare section of a strict reservation, whose scenery brings to the mind fantasy films about prehistoric times. There are mixed forest clusters of oak-tree and hornbeam, or of alder and ash, and many rare plant species. Local animal species include 300 European bisons, as well as elks, badgers, martens,

ermines, otters, deer, wild boars, lynxes and wolves. There are also rare birds, such as eagles, eagle owls, cranes and black storks. With a bit of luck, or an experienced guide, you may discover traces of primitive forest bee-keeping.

Unitl the 13th century, Białowieska Forest had been inhabited by the Jadźwing tribe. It was during the reign of King Władysław Jagiełło that it became part of the United Polish Kingdom and the Great Duchy of Lithuania. Great hunts had been the forest's tradition for hundreds of years. The most famous one was organised in 1732, by King August III.

Tourists are fascinated by the bisons, the tarpan horese (in a closed reservation,) the towering 50-metre-tall trees, the antique oaks, and the general atmosphere of a Europe long gone.

Hel Peninsula

The 35-kilometre-long and 0.5-3-kilometre-wide strip of land cutting into the sea, had been a chain of separate islands until as late as the 17th century. A popular tourist spot, it is invaded each summer by thousands of holiday-makers. Let us hope that the railway and the motorway that run along the peninsula will soon be closed – or the entire area will be trampled down by tourists and levelled by cars.

Hel Peninsula is full of legends. One of them has it that a prosperous fishing and trading village, Stary Hel, existed here even back in the 10th or 11th century. Whatever the truth, there is no questioning the fact that a township under that name was granted civic rights in 1378. And a hundred years later, Nowy Hel was built. Both townships used to belong to Gdańsk municipality.

The northernmost settlement of Hel Peninsula – once you have passed Władysławowo, Chałupy, Kuźnica, Jastarnia and Jurata – is Hel. With its

18th- and early 19th-century fishermen's houses, it looks more Danish or Dutch, than Polish – which it has always been.

In 1939, Hel resisted the Nazi invasion and was among the last bastions of defence to surrender in the September Campaign (on 2nd October.) The Commander of the Polish Fleet, Rear Admiral Józef Urung, had his headquarters here. In 1945, a group of nearly 100 thousand Nazi troops stationed in Hel were taken prisoners of war.

Nowhere in Poland is the marine climate as typical as in Hel. With the average annual temperature of 7.5°C, Poland's lowest temperature span (18.3°C) and modest rainfall, it is rather an exceptional spot.

Some of the Hel Peninsula dunes reach the height of 24 metres and resemble minor mountain ranges. There are two lighthouses on the peninsula: in Jastarnia and in Hel (the latter, shining with the power of 4 million candles, can be spotted 60 kilometres away.) Another lighthouse, in nearby Rozewie, hosts a unique Lighthouse History Museum.

The Kaszubian Switzerland

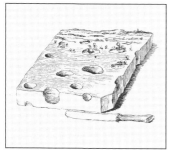

There are at least seven cities in Europe claiming the title of "Venice" (of the North, East or West.) Another five like to call themselves "Parises." The third most wanted geographical name – in Europe and beyond – is Switzerland.

Poland has several local Switzerlands. There is the Połczyńska Switzerland,

the Żerkowska Switzerland, as well as a Silesian forest and a Białystok region village, both by the same name. The major one, however, is the Kaszubian Switzerland in Pomerania district.

The area is, indeed, a mirror image of the real Switzerland. Its moraine hills of up to 200m, vast forests and numerous lakes of various sizes, had inspired a local patriot to compare it to William Tell's native country.

Will Tell himself never visited the region, unlike the Teutonic Knights and the Swedish (the latter rather less friendly in the past than they are now.) It is one of the most attractive tourist recreation areas in Poland. Its 250 lakes offer ample space for camping and sunbathing.

One of the region's major towns is Kościerzyna (21.4 thousand inhabitants,) a former castle-town of the Pomeranian Princes since 1284. The most popular tourist centre is Goluń, on Lake Wdzydze, with two typically Kaszubian houses turned into a local folk museum. Kalwaria in Wiel (on Lake Wieleńskie) boasts a neo-Baroque church of St. Nicholas, richly decorated with mural paintings. The local population of the Kaszub folk inhabit many parts of Gdańsk and Słupsk regions, as well as a number of small enclaves between lakes Łebsko and Gardno. The estimated 200,000 Polish Kaszubs are descendants of an autochtonous group of Slav Pomeranians. The region had always tempted its belligerent foreign neighbours, and the local population had been for ages subject to the pressures of germanization. However, the Gdańsk Kaszub folk have resisted the efforts, preserving their own, unique Polish dialect and some of their fascinating folklore.

Lake Pakoskie

Not far from Inowrocław, the brimming waters of Lake Pakoskie had sudden-

ly flooded its island supporting a massive fortified Slav castle-town. Some of the inhabitants managed to reach the mainland. The old castle-town stood deserted.

Twenty-five hundred years later, the water level dropped to reveal the flooded island. Archaeologists promptly rushed to examine the spot.

They discovered remains of old houses and fortifications, as well as objects of everyday use that must have been left behind by the escaping owners of the sinking houses, such as stone querns, horn hoes and spades, bone awls and etching needles, and some items of bronze jewellery.

To examine the structure of the castle-town, the scientists cut across it creating a deep, wide, 100-metre-long trench along the north-south axis. It revealed fragments of a breakwater and a palisade. Inside the castle walls, two rows of well-preserved houses were discovered. The houses were built of wooden logs and had clay floors. Some had open fireplaces, but others were equipped with clay-domed stoves, with a layer of broken pottery and stones serving as the grill. The houses stood in the area close to the castle walls. The empty central courtyard was paved with one to several layers of cobblestone. It is underneath the cobblestone that traces of the original Bronze-Age inhabitants of the island have been found. The archaeologists uncovered their living dens and storage pits. They also found some pottery that had been used by the ancient local people.

Some 50 kilometres away lies the castle-town of Biskupin – one of Poland's oldest relics of the Lusatian culture. The discoveries made on Lake Pakoskie island complete the picture of ancient Slav settlements in the area. Some experts claim that there are many more similar lake islands in Poland, bearing traces of the ancient life-styles.

Biskupin

If there had been no Biskupin, we the Slav people would not be what we are today. There would be no trace of our presence here in Europe thousand of years ago – the fact that was confirmed by the discovery of Biskupin, 50 kilometres from the modern Bydgoszcz.

The village that is probably Poland's most famous had been founded as a castle-town about 550 B.C. and recorded in unquestioned surviving documents. The castle-town stood on the then island measuring 200 by 160 metres, on Lake Biskupińskie. More than a hundred wooden houses were packed in 13 rows, along the 11 streets, surrounded with an earth-and-timber defence wall, complete with a double gate, a fortified watch tower and a 120-metre-long oakwood bridge. All these have survived to testify before the entire world that ancient Slav tribes had inhabited the area as early as the Hallstattan period. The survival was possible thanks to the marshy soil and partial silting that conserved not only the wooden parts of the buildings, but also many objects of common use.

The ancient settlement was discovered by sheer accident. It must have been a lucky day for the local teacher who, back in 1933, rather than correct students' papers, decided to take a walk along the lake and noticed something that nobody else had ever spotted before.

The settlement of Biskupin has been partly reconstructed and made a museum. Like all archaeological sites in the world, it is being continuously trampled down by groups and individual tourists. But wasn't it just the point of its excavation out of millenia-old dust?

The Birds at Milicz

A small 12th-century town of 12 thousand inhabitants – just the marketplace and a couple of streets – Milicz

lies to the north-east of Wrocław. The Barycz River – a tributary of the Oder – cuts across the poor local soils and lavish woods. The marshland on both sides of the Barycz has been a region of man-made fishing ponds since the Middle Ages, with the present total area of 6000 hectares, it is the largest artificially created water area in Europe.

Milicz has a unique micro-climate and a rich fauna. The local conditions are ideal for birds, especially water fowl. Though nearly identical with that of Mazury region, the fauna of Milicz area is confined to a considerably small territory, which makes it easier to observe. Milicz neighbourhood has become Poland's major ornithological watching grounds. The local "Milicz Reservoirs" bird reservation is under strict protection. Wrocław University has built an ornithological station in Milicz. It has been proposed that the area be given the status of an international reservation, like the Danube Delta.

It hosts Europe's largest population of greylag geese: the local 300 couples make up more than a half of all the greylags living in Poland. There are also two couples of the purple heron – the only ones in Poland until, recently, another pair was spotted on Lake Gopło. The nesting black stork is proof that the area is still wild. There is also a unique couple of the white eagles. Ornithologists from all over Europe visit the place to observe the biological cycles, the coexistence and the competition among the many bird species inhabiting the small territory. The British have made a half-hour documentary about Milicz birds.

For fear of any harm being done to their winged treasures, local authorities have battled down the project of building a chemical plant in the neighbourhood – a wise and laudable decision.

Visit Milicz – a place that still resounds with the gaggling of geese, rather than the roaring of automobiles.

Babia Góra

It is much more than just a single mountain. The southern region surrounding the local capital of Sucha Beskidzka is famous for its lavish greenery, crystalline air and landscapes of soothing beauty.

Babia Góra – the name meaning "Mount Old Wife" – is the centre of 1728-hectare Babiogórski National Park, an oasis of silence, full of rare plants and wildlife. The place attracts lovers of quiet relaxation and challenging tourism. The present local accommodation facilities may serve several thousand clients.

A new camping site and a tourist station have been built in Sucha, and the 18th-century wooden "Rome" inn is a major local attraction.

The town of Zawoja – a real beauty spot of the region – is still awaiting its big day. So far, it has been admired mainly by the guests of the 17 local youth-hostels and guest-houses, and by thousands of transit tourists on their way down south.

The highest peak of the Babia Góra Range is Diablak (Imp. 1725m.) connected with Mała Babia Góra [Mount Small Old Wife, 1517] by Brona Pass.

The local fir, beech and spruce forests are inhabited by deer and predatory lynxes; you may also meet some unusual birds – the black grouse and the wood grouse. As well as more and more

tourists – the majority of them, reportedly, female. *Nomen omen*: after all, this is Babia Góra – Mount Old Wife.

Sejny

A Polish borderland town, Sejny becomes noisy only during traditional local church fairs. It was the birthplace of a number of famous Poles, one of them being the nation's bravest woman – Emilia Plater. Nowadays, Sejny is famous for its interesting folklore, trade in sheep-skin coats and dried forest mushrooms, and, especially, for the local crayfish nursery, producing a million crustaceans a year. The surrounding Suwalskie Lake District is an area of great beauty, including one of Europe's loveliest lakes – Lake Wigry, crossed by River Czarna Hańcza. On the Wigry Peninsula stands Wigry Village – a one-time Cameldolite monastery with a Baroque church (built 1704–1745 by P. Putini) surrounded by the hermitages.

Many borderland villages run centres of Lithuanian folklore that are worth visiting. There is a multitude of fish, including some rare species, like the lavaret. Local natural reservations harbour beaver lodges.

You can still feel the pulse of the borderland Poland of decades ago in the region of Sejny.

Hitler's Headquarters

While millions of Germans fought and died on the fronts of World War II, their *Führer* sought peaceful refuges, far from the battlefields and military transport routes. He built one of his quiet nests in the Mazurian forest. It was a nest of steel and concrete. The hideout got the name of "The Woolf's Den."

The bunker, or what has remained of it, is situated 6 kilometres away from Kętrzyn, near Gierloż Village.

Until the Nazis blew it up in 1945, it had been the headquarters of the German military staff. It was there that the famous failed attempt at assassinating Hitler was tried, on 20 July, 1944.

The ruin of the killers' lair is now the only dissonance in the wonderfully harmonious landscape of north-eastern Poland that borders on the Great Mazury Lake District.

Hitler's Headquarters (or its surviving 50%) became the setting of a number of films; as well as a subject of many press articles and books. "The Woolf's Den" is now a tourist attraction, with a hotel and a restaurant. Many tourist groups visit it, young visitors listening in amazement to the tales of the awsome local history.

Allegedly, Hitler's last headquarters is believed to have been the one in Sowie Mountains, Wałbrzych neighbourhood: since 1997, tourists may visit the mysterious underground city that used to be the "Riese" military complex, consisting of numerous corridors and chambers cut out in the rock by prisoners of war.

The Forests

"The forest lived before us, the forest will live after us," tells an old Polish proverb, but it seems to have lost some of its actuality. The continued devastation of the environment makes no exception for forests, especially those growing in the upper areas.

Poland is still 28-percent overgrown with forests. At least ten of those vast wooded areas are classified as big forests: Kurpiowska (1800 km^2), Augustowska, Nadnotecka, Piska, Świętokrzyska, Bory Bydgosko-Tucholskie, Knyszyńska, Niepołomicka, Solska and Sandomierska forests.

In fact, only Białowieska and Piska forests fully deserve the big name. With the other ones, it is rather the question of tradition nowadays. Suffice it to say that Wkrzańska Forest stretches as far as... the centre of Szczecin.

There are, however, many woods of

moderate size, rich in uderbrush and wildlife, with an intense smell that can hardly be felt anywhere else in today's Europe.

In the beginning of its history, Poland was nearly all overgrown with dense forests. Industry has largely thinned them down, changing the proportions of the tree species, too. The number of the original larches, maples, ashes and, especially, mountain pines, has been diminishing, in favour of pine and spruce trees.

"Through thickets and forests, a soldier goes marching..." sang an old Polish song. Indeed, for centuries, a Pole usually meant a soldier, and marching across Poland usually implied tearing through forest thickets.

All over the world, ancient thickets and forests are being gradually replaced with concrete and asphalt. Poland has still preserved some of its forest substance, but even this is being threatened by "acid rains" and other fruit of civilizational progress.

Small Towns

The 16th century Poland was a country of as many as 700 towns. However, only eight of them boasted a population of more than 10 thousand. The present number of urban settlements is not much higher, there being 826 towns and cities, but as many as 42 have over 100 thousand inhabitants. Few Polish towns have developed as fast as Łódź, or as several centres in Silesia. There are towns that have preserved their population statistics almost unchanged for many centuries, focused on conserving their respective historic architectures.

Big cities usually tend to look the same – it is the small towns that cultivate their otherness. Tourists are advised to visit some of the 254 urban units that have not made great modernizing careers.

Starting your tour at ex-municipalities, like Czersk or Wiślica, you may sadly observe a past glory. Therefore, we rather recommend towns like Biecz, Lwówek Śląski, Łęczyca, Rydzyna, Chełmno nad Wisłą, Pińczów, Jarosław, Pułtusk, Kalisz (the famous Calisia that was one of the first towns on the Polish map.) Rawicz, Stary Sącz, or Leszno. There are also the charming little towns of Greater Poland, Lower Silesia and Pomerania. It is certainly best to be born in the countryside, work in a big city, and make your home in Biecz or in Stary Sącz.

Baranów

Film-makers are looking for a good setting for shooting a lavish feast, or a duel in a fine, arcaded courtyard will come down to Baranów. There, they may find an authentic 16th-century archtecture and atmosphere.

Specialists call Baranów (12 kilometres away from Tarnobrzeg, not far from Sandomierz) a "mannerist" castle. To a layman, the term may (unjustly) sound slightly pejorative, in discord with the information that the castle has been listed among the champions of world historical monuments. As early as the 17th century, Szymon Starowolski extolled Baranów, calling it *elegantissima*, with arcades, Renaissance attics and portals unparallelled for miles around. Today, Baranów Castle is sometimes called "the little Wawel."

The successive owners of Baranów were noble Polish families of Leszczyński, Wiśniowiecki, Lubomirski,

Sanguszko, Krasicki and Dolański. The castle's architect is unknown, but Baranów may have been built (1591–1606) by the Italian architect and sculptor, Santi Gucci. The 17th-century renovations of the first-floor interiors in the Baroque style were directed by the famous Tylman of Gameren.

Two big fires and the Second World War have done considerable damage to the "little Wawel's" beauty. State-appropriated after the War, it went through complex renovations that returned it to its former splendour. All the castle halls and chambers were fully furnished. The immediate supervisor of the works was the neighbouring Tarnobrzeg sulphur factory: they did not miss the chance to organise inside it an archaeological-geological exhibition, with sulphur as the main motive.

Next door to the castle, in the beautiful park, a recommendable hotel has been built. Visitors will be relieved to know that no traces of the White Lady, or of any other local ghost, have been reported.

The Spas

Polish spas have traditionally enjoyed great popularity. Millions of people seem to trust the beneficial influence of mineral waters, mud baths and micro-climates.

Since before the War, one of the most popular Polish spas has been Krynica. It has hosted the Dutch Queen Juliana and her husband, Prince Bernard, and Jan Kiepura – the world-famous Polish tenor – used to be its citizen. Krynica is still Poland's major spa, as well as an important sports centre.

Some waters of the Polish spas are said to be the most potent in Europe. This is true of the springs of Szczawno Zdrój (for those who suffer from respiratory, metabolic and digestive disorders,) Busko Zdrój and Ciecho-

cinek (rheumatic, children's, gynaecological and skin diseases,) Krynica (digestive, urinary, gynaecological, circulatory malfunctions, and diabetes,) and Kudowa (anaemia, hormonal disorders – especially of the thyroid, circulatory problems,) Other popular spas include: Iwonicz, Rymanów, Cieplice, Rabka, Połczyn, Świeradów, Żegiestów, Polanica, Nałęczów, Duszniki, Lądek and Kołobrzeg.

Ciechocinek is unique with its saline waters concentrated in graduation towers (a technology proposed by Stanisław Staszic.) The spa was founded in 1836. Polish spas were recorded, in Polish-language documents, as early as 1578, by Wojciech Oczko who mentioned, among other places, Iwonicz, Lubień and Swoszowice.

Poland has 36 functioning spas and 25 centres classified as demi-spas.

Dębno

Fourteen kilometres away from Nowy Targ, lies a mountain village, rich in historic local architecture, with one treasure object of European importance. It is a small wooden church, one of the oldest examples of sacral folk architecture. Although its name was recorded as early as the 13th century, the little church is officially classified as a 15th-century construction. Its walls and ceilings are decorated with polychrome of ca. 1500. The imaginative originality and vivid colouring of the murals are truly amazing. The church also contains 14th and 15th-century sculptures. There may be even more precious items, still undiscovered, like the oldest Polish easel painting – a Romanesque painting on wood of 1330 – which was found by sheer accident, in 1949.

An eminent collector of European folk art told the Author of this book: "If I could decide, I'd like to die in the Dębno church and be buried in the local cemetery."

Gniezno

An 8th-century settlement is known to have stood on Mount Lech – a hill that, since the 10th century, had supported the first capital of Piast dynasty princes. It was also here that King Bolesław Chrobry met Emperor Otto III, in the year 1000 – a historical event of major importance, since it led to establishing the Archbishopric at Gniezno.

Bolesław was the first man to be called "Polish" by the old chronicles. In 1025, he was crowned Poland's king. Gniezno Cathedral (built in the 14th-15th-century) includes fragments of a pre-Romanesque (10th-century) and a Romanesque (11th-century) cathedrals, and is rich in historical treasures, e.g. the Wit Stwosz-sculpted tombstone of Primate Zbigniew Oleśnicki, other Gothic, Renaissance and Baroque gravestones, tombs, statues and Baroque altars.

The 12th-century bronze Gniezno Portal, composed of 18 horizontal rectangular plates featuring the legend of St. Adalbert [Wojciech] – his life, missionary activity and martyrdom – are among the masterpieces of Romanesque decorative art.

Other local places of interest include: St. George's Church (13th-century) St. John's Church (14th-century) the archaeological museum, and a number of old tenements.

The town and its neighbourhood have been scenes of many a bloody battle. Several years ago, a ruthless robber damaged and stole a fragment of the silver coffin from the Baroque tomb of St. Adalbert. The thief was captured and the historic object is now reconstructed.

The name "Gniezno" is justly associated with the modern Polish meaning of *gniazdo* ("a nest".) The place was, indeed, one of the original nests of the Slav Polan tribe.

Legend has it that it was here that Lech, the legendary local ruler, discovered the nest of a white eagle and promptly made the noble bird the emblem of his Polan tribe. The story gives Gniezno an additional meaning. The town of 55,000 inhabitants lies not far (51km) from Poznań. It has a truly fascinating history and offers some unique documents.

Częstochowa

A city of almost 300 thousand, Częstochowa boasts a developing industry and rich cultural life. But visitors' attention is focused on the local monastery, situated on top of Jasna Góra [Luminous Mountain] hill.

The Pauline monastery with the famous Gothic icon of Our Lady of Częstochowa – also known in the world as the Black Madonna – is the major object of Polish Catholic cult and the destination of countless pilgrimages.

Jasna Góra has a rich history. It has entered literature (Henryk Sienkiewicz's *The Deluge*) and has given rise to many legends. One of its famous historic figures was Father Augustyn Kordecki, the Pauline abbot who successfully defended the monastery, in 1655, against a massive attack of the Swedish General Muller troops, commanding an army of local peasants and townsfolk. The brave monk later recorded his feat in a diary, slightly exaggerating his own role and the strategic importance of the operation. Jasna Góra Monastery was founded in 1382 and fortified some 300 years later. Its strenght was tried again at the end of the last War, during the withdrawal of the Nazi troops. The SS had mined the monastery church with powerful explosives, setting the detonator to delayed action. The church with the miraculous Madonna was meant to explode as soon as it was entered by the Red Army troops.

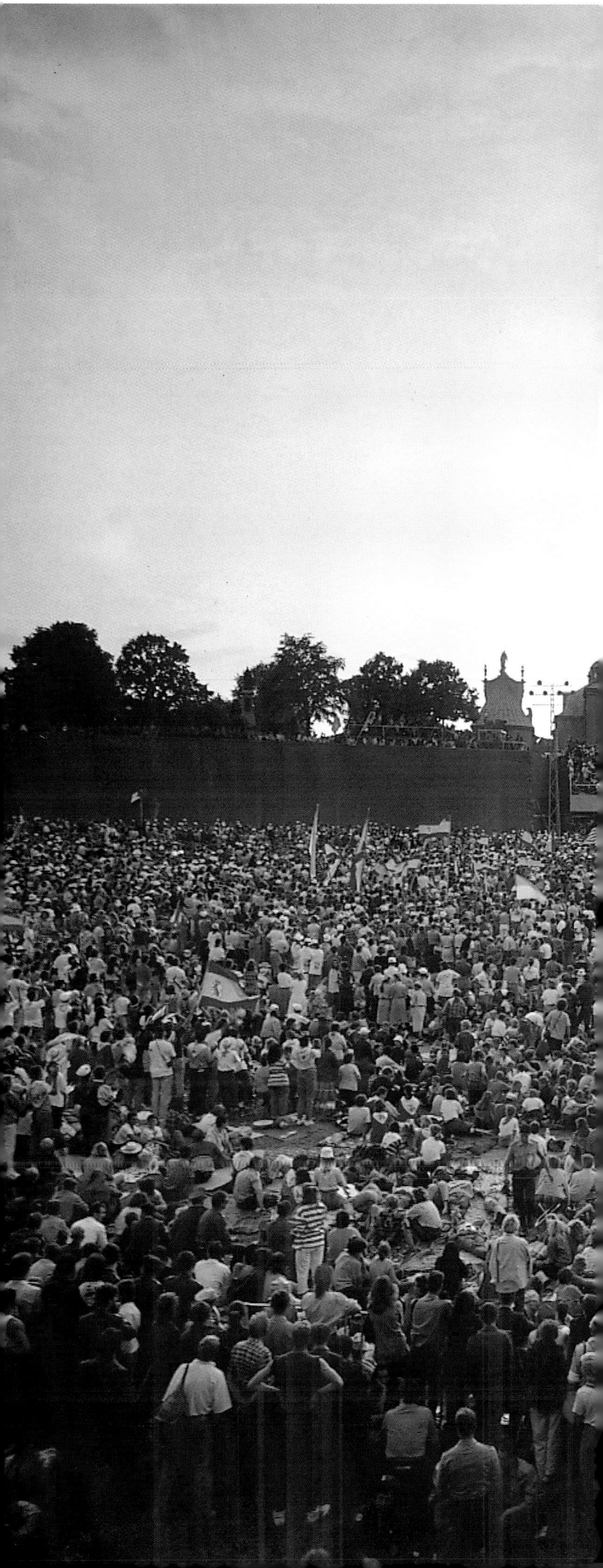

The Black Madonna

Frombork, the cathedral church

Luckily, the explosives were removed in time to prevent the tragedy.

The thirty-six air-borne bombs were taken out and dismantled. The search revealed two detonators: a shock one, placed within the entrance as a trap, and a chemical one that was supposed to go off after ten days.

Back to the monastery, our attention is drawn by the soaring 15th-century Gothic church, rebuilt in the 17th century to become a basilica, with a richly ornamented Baroque interior, including the magnificent high altar (1726.) To its left, in the 15th-century Gothic chapel, hangs the famous Black Madonna, encased in the ebony and silver of the altar frame. There is also the monastery treasury, the Knights' Hall with a collection of paintings and a library, Poland's oldest functioning printing press, the arsenal and the royal chambers. The church tower is 105 metres high: it must have offered a perfect view of the enemy armies that invaded Częstochowa.

The successive occupats of Jasna Góra never dared to openly desecrate the place. Even in Communist times, despite the many intrigues, pressures and blackmailing attempts that were meant to dissuade the pilgrims from visiting Częstochowa, an open attack on the national shrine was never tried. Unless we count the authorities' decision to build a huge steelworks complex in the immediate neighbourhood, named after Communist president Bierut.

During the 1980s, Częstochowa gathered "Solidarność" people, for prayers and clandestine meetings. Jasna Góra has been visited by many heads of state and international celebrities; Pope John Paul II has been there several times.

Foreign corespondents often send home astonished reports of million-strong crowds at Jasna Góra.

Frombork

While the wonderful architecture of Frombork can be admired on the spot, the most precious local movables have to be looked for in Sweden where they were deported in 1626 by King Gustav Adolph.

The majority of the town's modest population of 2.6 thousand are engaged in the local fishing industry. In summer, Frombork hosts as many tourists as it has inhabitants.

The major local place of interest is the fortified cathedral complex, and especially the cathedral itself, built in the 14th century by the Warmia Chapter. But Frombork owes its fame mainly to Nicholas Copernicus who lived and worked here from 1512 until his death in 1543, writing his monumental thesis, *De revolutionibus orbium coelestium*.

Every second object in Frombork bears the name of the genius astronomer, to mention only Copernicus Hill and Copernicus Tower.

Grunwald

Several geographical names associated with major historical events have entered common speech. They are names like Canossa, Waterloo, or Hiroshima. In Polish, the word "Grunwald" signifies a major victory. The Germans call the place Tannenberg and proudly associate it with the events of 1914, when the German 8th Army commanded by Hindenburg beat the Russian 2nd Army of General Samsonov.

The Battle of Grunwald was fought on 15 July, 1410. Joint Polish, Lithuanian and Russian forces, commanded by King Władysław Jagiełło, won a triumphant victory over the army of the Teutonic Knights. The Grand Master of the Teutonic Order and his elders were killed in the battle that shaped the future of Central and Eastern Europe for many years to come.

Today, the battlefield at Grunwald can be approached by an asphalt road, flashy signs pointing the way. On the 550th anniversary of the great battle, the spot was honoured with the Monument to Grunwald Victory (designed by Jerzy Bandura.) The monument includes an amphitheatre, facing a granite mosaic that features the positions of the opposing army before the battle.

The Battle of Grunwald has inspired writers (Henryk Sienkiewicz, *The Teutonic Knights*) painters (Jan Matejko, *The Battle of Grunwald*), and filmmakers. The results were all "grunwalds" for their authors.

Kórnik

Kórnik is one of those small, off-the-main-road Polish towns, that hold many hidden surprises.

Situated 20 kilometres from Poznań, it offers unusual buildings, books and trees. Its major pride is the castle with its collections of portraits, old-Polish armours, Oriental weapons, antique furniture, as well as natural and ethnological exhibits from Australia, Polynesia, Madagascar and... Kórnik neighbourhood. There is also a library with 150 thousand volumes, including the manuscripts of Adam Mickiewicz and Juliusz Słowacki.

Last but not least, there are the trees in the stylish local park – Poland's largest dendrological garden that has been made Arboretum of the Polish Academy of Science. It contains 10 thousand trees and shrubs, both home-grown and exotic.

Indeed, the small town of Kórnik can satisfy varied interests.

Until the late 16th-century, Kórnik was owned by the powerful Górka family. It was later taken over by the Działyńskis, and, finally, by the Zamojskis. The last owners have recently held a long-postponed family reunion in Kórnik Castle.

Łańcut

Łańcut Palace is probably the most visited provincial museum in Poland. Its magnificent Interior Decoration Museum vies for popularity with the Horse-Carriage Museum – part of the palace complex that, while not too rich in exhibits, successfully boosts the visitors' imagination with tangible synbols of days gone by.

The palace is early-Baroque, quadrilateral, with an inner courtyard and four corner towers. It was designed by Maciej Trapola and built in 1629–1641. In 1954, the bulding underwent major renovations.

Łańcut Palace is counted among the most magnificent magnate residences in East and Central Europe. A vast part of its originally vast collection that used to occupy 300 palace chambers, was shipped abroad in 11 railway carriages by the palace's last custodian, Alfred Potocki, in July, 1944. After the War, only a small part of it could be won back; however, the interiors have been successfully recreated and the palace chambers glitter again with the splendour of hictorical furniture, porcellain, tapestries, paintings and sculptures.

The Horse-Carriage Museum was started in the 1920s. Its collection of fifty-plus carriages includes coaches, chaises, wagonettes, hunting carts and stage-coaches from the 18th to the early 20th century.

Since 1961, Łańcut has hosted famous music festivals and celebrity concerts.

The palace is surrounded by a beautiful park, its paths shaded by ancient lime, oak and poplar trees (one of the poplars measures 9 metres in circumference.) The statue-adorned conservatory grows many exotic plants, orchids included, that are shipped to flowershops all over the country.

Many original 18th and 19th-century

buildings have survived in the neighbouring villages, where you can still meet some active local folk sculptors, while the villages of Medynia and Zalesie make the country's biggest folk pottery centre.

At the turn of the 17th century, Łańcut was owned by the ill-famous villain and troublemaker Stanisław Stadnicki who earned himself the nickname of "Łańcut Devil." The place has seen several other devils since; some – according to a local park warden – take on the shapes of tourists.

setting free its inmates, among them Polish General Olbrycht "Olza" – all in broad daylight.

The local Bernardinian monastery complex – another object of all the pilgrimages – is certainly worth visiting. Its church was built in 1603–1609 by Paulus Baudarth and Giovanni Bernardoni. It includes a silver statue of Our Lady, bought in Rome in the 16th century, as well as 15th and 16th-century liturgical robes, 18 Polish incunabula, and other precious items.

Kalwaria Zebrzydowska

There are at least five different Kalwarias in Poland, apart from Góra Kalwaria and several other places of related names. The most important one, however, is Kalwaria Zebrzydowska, a town lying 34 kilometres from Krakow, a famous vast, mannerist-Baroque centre of Chruch Indulgence fetes. Pilgrims flock to Kalwaria Zebrzydowska, especially in August (one of the pilgrimages has become the subject of a demascatory documentary, ruthlessly revealing "Dark Age" aspects of the event.)

To the south and east of the town, among the surrounding hills and valleys, stretches a unique object of landscape architecture: the Way of the Cross, composed of 42 Baroque and mannerist churches and chapels, most of them designed by Paulus Baudarth. The spectacular religious performances that are organised in Kalwaria resemble those held in southern Spain.

Kalwaria Zebrzydowska is also a renowned furniture-making centre, active since the 18th century. There are some 500 joiners working in the little town.

In 1944, Kalwaria became the scene of a sensational war episode. A Home Army partisan group took hold of the town and demolished the local prison,

Kazimierz Dolny

It is almost like a distant suburb of Warsaw. With two good motorways – especially the charming road along the Vistula bank – and few villages on the way, the 130-kilometre journey feels short.

The "Kazimierz Equation" is simple: wonderful situation + historical monuments = good entertainment.

Kazimierz Dolny (there are more towns in Poland called Kazimierz) has often been used as the setting of films whose actions take place in... southern Europe. The local market-place, surrounded by Renaissance tenements, the parish church revealing fragments of 14th-century walls, the stone castle ruin, the church and monastery perched on a lovely hill, the 17th-century corn-houses by the river (the one that burnt down in 1972 has now been reconstructed) – the entire

Kazimierz Dolny, the Market-place

The Stołowe Mountains

urban complex is reminiscent of Italy, and still unmistakeably Polish.

In spring, when fruit trees bloom on the slopes of Kazimierz hills, the little town off the main driving routes becomes a sheer paradise on earth. This, anyway, is the opinion of painters, photographers and lovers.

The cobblestone area of the Market-place allows no cars.

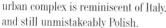
Kłodzko

The regional capital of Kłodzka Valley is situated on the Nysa Kłodzka River. Kłodzko is a monument-town, one of Silesia's oldest settlements, mentioned by chronicles since the year 981 as a borderland stronghold. In the 11th and the 12th centuries, it was several times occupied by the Czech. Regained for Poland by the Piast rulers in 1278, the area was conquered again by the Czech in 1341, in the meantime (c.13) having fallen under Prussia.

Despite all those odds, Kłodzko remained a principally Polish town. Even in the 18th century, local civic documents were printed in the Polish language. And it is in Kłodzko that one of the oldest Polish-language texts was produced, i.e. the 14th-century *Psałterz floriański*.

The most spectacular local historical monument is the Gothic stone bridge, built between 1281 and 1390 and later supplied with Baroque statues to resemble the famous Charles Bridge in Prague. Other monuments include: a Gothic parish church (c.15th) with a rich Baroque interior, the town-hall (c.17th) with a Renaissance tower, and a number of tenements with Renaissance and Baroque façades. The entire town is dominated by a looming, vaulted stronghold, built in the 17th century and expanded during the occupation of Silesia by Prussian King Frederic II. Kłodzka Valley is a picturesque region, with specific climactic and natural conditions. An area of a mere 500

square kilometres, it contains several mountain ranges of exotic names, such as Sowie [Owl], Bardzkie [Bard], Złote [Gold] and Stołowe [Table] Mountains; deep, but unkempt, mostly deciduous forests, and many Europe-famous spas with mineral water springs (Kudowa, Duszniki, Polanica, Lądek, Długopole, etc.)

Kłodzko was one of the victims of the violent floods that swamped Lower Silesia in 1997.

Krasiczyn

According to some experts, the proud and perfectly located Krasiczyn Castle is not so much a construction, as... a comment. "Krasiczyn Castle is for us a fantastic example of architecture employed as a political and social comment," wrote Professor Stanisław Lorentz. "Its symbolism refers to a Polish political treatise of the second half of the 16th century, that defended Counterreformation and proposed the first draft of the national Sarmatian philosophy."

However, to the modern visitors of Krasiczyn, the castle is definitely an architectural object, rather than a "comment" of any kind. Still, it is impossible to ignore the meaningful names of the four rounded towers: Lordly, Royal, Papal and Divine. The spacious walls are covered in Renaissance Lombardy-style sgraffito, featuring medallions with the busts of the Roman emperors.

Krasiczyn was built in 1592–1614, largely by Galeazo Appiani. It is a quadrilateral, square edifice, with an inner arcaded courtyard. A variety of attics add to its unusual beauty.

The fairy-tale construction of the castle is surrounded by a vast, 20-hectare, typical 19th-century park, its lavish greenery and trees invading on the buildings.

Might all current political comments look like that!

Kazimierz Dolny

Książ

In southern Poland's Wałbrzych neighbourhood stands another seemingly fairy-tale castle: huge, old, mysterious and allegedly packed with ghosts.

A Piast Prince, Bolko I Świdnicki, had it built in 1292, on the Pełcznica River. In later years, the construction was often rebuilt (especially in the 16th, 18th and 19th centuries) and redecorated. Its last owners before World War II were the Dukes of Pszczyna.

The present 160-cubic-metre construction has 400 castle chambers and 200 office rooms. It is surrounded by a wonderful park, with rhododendrons, two artificial ponds and one natural lake.

In 1941, the Germans tried to convert the castle into one of Hitler's residences. They even started drilling in the foundations to build monstrous bunkers, thus destroying vast portions of the wonderful interiors. It was not until recently that the last huge dent in the front of the castle was filled, to level the creative efforts of Todt's organisation.

Its lofty position on top of a hill makes the castle very photogenic. No wonder it was used as the film setting for *The Duchess Cosel*.

Reconstruction of the ruined and devastated castle is a huge project that has been taken up by several joint institutions and organisations.

Książ is one of the chain of Lower Silesian castles, the others being Grodno, Bolków, Siedlęcin, Wlenia and Lwówka. The only missing element is the connecting Loire River.

Łagów

One of the Polish towns whose administrative status has been reduced to village, Łagów still prospers, offering charming landscapes and rich heritage to thousands of visitors.

For nearly 500 years, it had been a seat of the wealthy Order of St. John whose knights contributed a lot to the region's development, especially by building a castle. Its 14th-century construction was later rebuilt several times. There is a Gothic vaulted hall on the ground floor and a collection of armours. The Medieval castle tower offers a splendid panorama of the town and its surroundings. The castle has now been leased to the Henryk Wieniawski Poznań Musical Society and is used by the artists as a recreation centre. Locally organised Lubuskie Film Summer meetings – originally a Polish film festival – have gained considerable fame as an international film-makers' jamboree.

Łagów claims to be the brightest pearl of Lubusz County – an area on both sides of the middle Oder, between Silesia and Pomerania. There is evidence of the region's having been Polish even back in the times of Mieszko I. In 1124, King Bolesław Krzywousty established the bishopric in Lubusz. Soon after that, in 1250, Lubusz County fell into the hands of the Brandenburg margraves who made it their buffer of expansion towards Silesia, Greater Poland and Pomerania. In 1945, the part of Lubusz County east of the Oder was returned to Poland. Its present regional capital is Zielona Góra.

One of the big old city gates of Łagów had been named by its constructors the Polish Gate: the name has never been changed, not even under the German rule.

The "village" spreads along the isthmus between lakes Ciecz and Łagowskie, surrounded by hills and forests.

Malbork

Malbork is a town of 40 thousand inhabitants. But, above all else, Malbork is a castle.

Malbork Castle is among the top ten of the Polish sightseeing "musts".

A magnificent example of Medieval fortifications, it was originally the seat of the Grand Master of the Teutonic Knights Order.

The Forecastle, also called the Lower Castle, includes: the armoury, the bell-foundry, St. Laurence's Chapel, Maślankowa [Buttertop] Tower, and the walls of a Gothic hamlet. The Middle Castle used to house the offices of the High Commander, the hospital, the knights' hall and the palace of the Grand Master. The High Castle included: the chapter hall, the treasury, the bedrooms, the "golden gate," the Order's refectory, and the central water-well in the courtyard.

The biggest castle complex in 13th-14th-century Europe, Malbork become, since the 15th century, one of the main seats of the Polish kings. The Teutonic Knights' castle, whose looming bulk resembles at dusk a surrealist decoration for a horror film, has been carefully restored from the War-time damage, and the almost totally ruined Malbork Old Town has been reconstructed.

Nieborów and Arcadia

All tourist guidebooks describe Nieborów Palace as "magnificent." A masterpiece designed by Dutch architect Tylman von Gameren, it has successfully braved the storms of nearly three centuries, to become a branch of the venerable National Museum of Warsaw.

The palace was originally built in Baroque style and supplied with an exquisite garden.

The word "magnificent" is especially true of the palace interiors which contain: an interesting collection of majolica, a valuable library with numerous old prints, a staircase whose walls are inlaid with umpteen thousand Delft tiles, period furniture, a portrait gallery, as well as a collection of ancient sculptures, including the famous Niobe head that had inspired poet Konstanty Ildefons Gałczyński – a frequent visitor to Nieborów and its faithful admirer – to write his great poem:

Just like that lamp in Nieborów that he had sat under,
watching the face of Niobe, Niobe of Nieborów.
Sparks from the chandelier skipped along the roof-beams
and November was coming, soiled boots on its feet,
a maple leaf in its hair,
sun crumbs in its heart.

Gałczyński was one of the many artists, writers and scientists who made their second homes in Nieborów after it had been proclaimed a "creative study centre" for artists and art historians. A special pavillion was built to accommodate them. Cardinal-Archbishop Michał Radziejowski and other aristocratic owners of the palace, were thus succeeded in Nieborów by an aristocracy of the quill, the stage and the easel – as well as by crowds of foreign tourists.

It was in Nieborów Park that Henryk Sienkiewicz got the idea of Lygia – the heroine of his Nobel Prize-winning novel, *Quo Vadis.*

Four kilometres away is Arcadia – a Romantic-pastoral landscape park („magnificent," too) complete with stylish gazebos, grottoes and statues. The park's was designed proposed in 1773, by Lady Helen Radziwiłł.

Not far from Warsaw (89 kilometres.) Nieborów and Arcadia is an oasis of peace and beauty, suspended in time and space. Or, as Gałaczyński preferred to say: *Seeing the library globes, the Moon would linger / to trace the Mediterranean with its silver finger.*

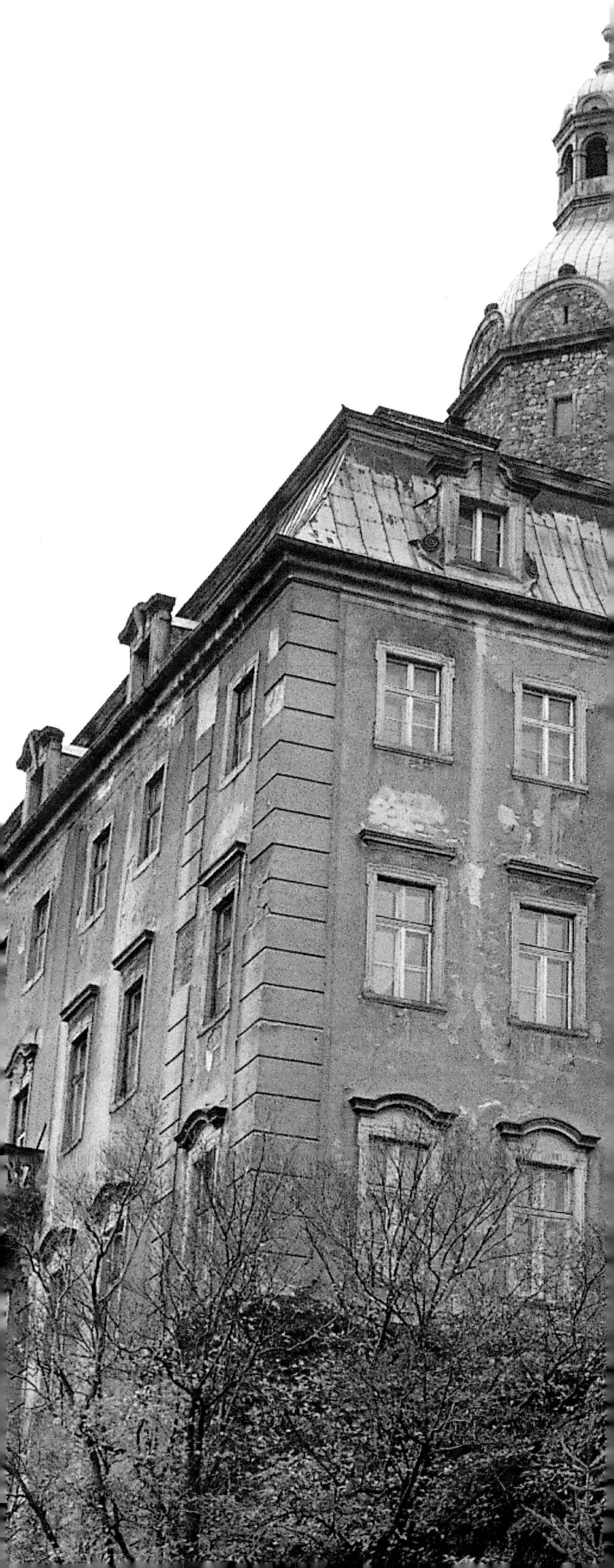

Sandomierz

Chroniclers mentioned this town as early as the 11th century. A centre of considerable importance, Sandomierz has never been fortune's favourite: it was twice damaged by the Tartars, fell victim of a sweeping 17th-century epidemic, became target of the Swedish invasion, and, more recently, was made an arena of military operations in both the World Wars.

Despite all those odds, Sandomierz has kept much of its past glory. Local guidebooks reccommend visiting the Cathedral (1382); the home of chronicler Jan Długosz (1478); the Dominican Church (1226); St. Paul's Church (1434); the Baroque Benedictine Sisters' convent and church, and the Renaissance Town-hall.

But the most wonderful things cannot be catalogued, such as the atmosphere of a Medieval borough, present in this wonderfully green town, splendidly situated on a lofty river-bank.

The town's wonderful location is, at the same time, its curse: the steep escarpment that is being continuously undermined by water, threatens to crumble. Architects and restorers are constantly on the alert. Following some serious damages of the recent years, major reconstruction and satefy operations are now being conducted, also in the market-place.

Sandomierz has become a Mecca for tourists, especially of the younger generations, and for artists. On nice summer days, there are sometimes more visitors than local inhabitants.

Sandomierz was the home town of Poland's major Renaissance composer Mikołaj Gomółka (c.16th) and of the eminent historian Jan Długosz (c.15th)

Writer Stefan Żeromski described Sandomierz in his novel *The Ashes* and Jarosław Iwaszkiewicz often mentioned it in his own novels and poems.

Pieskowa Skała

The picturesque territory of the ancient Wiślanie tribe country deserves a thorough exploration. An area of unending new historical discoveries, it challenges tourists with a painstaking task of seeing all that has already been discovered.

All around Krakow and along the Vistula bank, stretches an area of undulating hills. There is the Prądnik stream running deep in at the bottom of a steep gorge. There is also Ojców National Park, with a rocky cliff of Pieskowa Skała [Sand Rock] supporting a castle.

This Gothic castle of the 14th century, was later rebuilt in late-Gothic and Renaissance styles, to acquire its present shape of a stylish Gothic-Renaissance edifice that houses a branch of the Wawel National Arts Collection.

Pieskowa Skała is ranked among the most beautiful fortified castles in Poland, boasting a 16th-century arcaded courtyard, 21 gargoyles, bastion fortifications and a 56-metre-deep water-well. The castle was built as a stronghold for King Kazimierz the Great. Later, it changed owners and was, until 1608, the property of the Szafraniec family whose several members were known as prosperous highwaymen (no wonder, having such a great hideout,) as well as part-time alchemists: this may explain the name of the nearby Sokola Skała [Falcon Rock,] also known as Maczuga Herkulesa [Hercules' Cudgel,] associated with the legend of Master Twardowski.

Out of the many similar fortified objects that had surrounded Krakow, only the famous castles of Niepołomice and Wiśnicz have survived to this day, the one at Ogrodzieniec having been demolished.

Looking at the thick walls, the massive towers and the strong gates, one may easily imagine the armoured

knights galloping in and out on their armoured horses.

The Ghosts

Although the majority of famous ghosts and phantoms (i.e. antipathetic ghosts) prefer to live (?) in the castles and palaces of Great Britain, some have chosen other countries – provided that they offer proper accommodation that agrees with their supernatural tastes.

Not as fearsome as the living, ghosts are a real delight to all sound rationalists. On a clear night, we recommend a trip to Bolków Castle hill, where you can meet the shadow of the ill-fated clown who accidentally killed King Bolesław II's only son with a stone, and was promptly beheaded. And at the Lubomirski castle at Wiśnicz Nowy (Bochnia neighbourhood), once the most magnificent Polish magnate castle, you may have some inspiring encounters with phantoms of thieves who were murdered during their attempted robberies of the castle treasures. Toszek Castle in Upper Silesia offers a chance to see (especially in the guest rooms) an ethereal figure in white. And the "Red Phantom" (believed to have been a blood-thirsty *raubritter*) haunts the castle of Grodziec, near Złotoryja. A choice of fine, nasty nightmares awaits all those who would dare to doze off at the top floor of the excellently restored Szydłowiec castle. And the ruins of one of Europe's largest castles, in Ogrodzieniec, near Zawiercie, have been nightly haunted by a huge phantom of a black dog, dragging a long, ominously rattling chain. Phantom residents are also quite common in top-class world heritage monuments. The famous Łańcut Palace offers quite a choice of local ghosts, with the "Blue Lady," a woman in white (always scribbling something at her Rococo writing pulpit), and a male figure, dressed in a Polish nobleman's costume, believed to be Stanisław Stadnicki – the "Łańcut Devil," immortalized in one of the portraits: not only does the Devil step out of the picture frame, but he is also wont to gallop on a horse along Łańcut's paths, shrouded in a black cape. The Radziwiłł palace at Nieborów – especially the library room – is the haunting grounds of Cardinal Michał Radziejowski (who used to haunt Poland even in his lifetime.) Krasiczyn Castle – one of the country's finest – boasts the phantom of a young maiden who had jumped off the castle tower to avoid an unwelcome marriage, and was doomed to wander around on hot July nights. A similar phantom has been recorded in Werynia, a former Tyszkiewicz family palace. The excellently preserved 15th-century fortified castle at Dębno, off the Kraków-Tarnów road, has been troubled by the weeping and whinig of a 15-year-old female ghost whose live body had been sealed in the wall by a cruel father. Wilanów Palace has its own tenants from the beyond.

Poland is teeming with the ghosts of its many castles. Night after night, the "Black Lady" roams the ruined tower at Lesko, the loud giggles of the "Little Lady" resound in Odrzykoń Castle near Krosno, the "Harsh Lady" walks the arcades of the Renaissance castle at Sucha Beskidzka, while the "Good Lady" is active in Bobolice Castle, in Myszków neighbourhood.

More phantoms inhabit the castles of Olsztyn (the local governor, leader of a 16th-century rebellion against the King); Reszel, Olsztyn province, (a witch burnt on the stake); Wenecja, in Żnin neighbourhood, (the "Venetian Devil" mentioned by the great poet Mickiewicz); Kórnik (another white lady – this one enjoying the company of a mounted knight), and Krzyżtopór at Ujazd near Opatów, whose ruins are

frequented by a wing-rustling hussar officer on horseback.

Many volumes have been written on Polish demonology. Experts penetrate the hair-raising domain to boost national glory and amuse the visitors. Believe it – or not!

Przemyśl

A central Polish town for centuries, Przemyśl has been relegated to the country's eastern borderland, following the shift of the national borders after World War II.

Przemyśl has been there "since Adam" – an important trading post on the Krakow-Kijów, or (as some might prefer) the Europe-Asia route. There are documents confirming its existence even in the first millenium. And as early as the 10th century, the place was a Jewish merchant colony and a busy Polish-Russian trading centre. However, commerce was soon endangered by the town's strategic location that attracted less peaceful visitors: Przemyśl was successively raided by Russ and Hungarian hordes, followed (since c.17th) by the Tartars, the Cossacks, the Swedish, and again the Hungarians, as well as, in more recent times, the Austrians, the Germans and the Russians.

At the critical point, wars and epidemics reduced the population to 1700 persons. The powerful 15th and 16th-century fortifications, with high walls and deep moats, ten keeps and three gates, proved insufficient as a military defence system. However, modern tourists find them impressive enough. Przemyśl is ranked among the most beautiful Polish towns. Situated on terrace hills overlooking the River San, it boasts a Medieval urban complex of great historical value that, luckily, has survived in its original shape.

Tourist guidebooks compete in lengthening the list of the local places of interest. All recommend visiting the castle (built for many years since 1340) which has retained its original magnificence, despite the many demolitions and reconstructions it had gone through. Fragments of a rotunda and a palace built at the turn of the 11th century, have been recently discovered on the site. For the last 110 years, the castle has been the address of the nonprofessional Aleksander Fredro Drama Society "Fredreum" [named so to commemorate the great Polish playwright of the 19th century.]

Apart from the castle, Przemyśl boasts a cathedral, recently proclaimed basilica, of St. John the Baptist: its construction took centuries (the final shape was reached in the 15th–16th centuries, but the foundations had been laid in the early 11th century) and the original Gothic building was partly rebuilt in Baroque style. It includes late Gothic sculptures, Renaissance tombstones, late Baroque polychrome, and other treasures of European art.

There are also the old monastic complexes of the Order of St. Francis and the Barefoot Carmelites, both decorated by Polish and Italian masters; and the Baroque Clock Tower, as well as the arcaded tenements of the Market-place.

Przemyśl – just like the rest of southeastern Poland – is predominantly Baroque, full of churches, palaces (Łańcut!), castles and old tenements. Some wonderful Orthodox icons have survived in local Roman-Catholic, Greek-Catholic and Orthodox churches, and an imposing collection of icons is on display at the National Museum of Przemyśl Region. There are also many folk sculptures and roadside "Pensive Christ" figures. Church bells ring all around: no wonder the bell-casting museum found its quarters in Przemyśl Clock Tower.

Przemyśl has had many outstanding visitors, one of them being the Brave

Soldier Shveik himself, arrested in Przemyśl for one of his "brilliantly cretinous tricks."

For some time after the War, the Przemyśl community felt offended for having been deprived of the leading role in the province, as the regional administrative centre was shifted to Rzeszów. It is easier to understand the resentment if we remember that Przemyśl had been one of Poland's oldest towns (c.10th) as well as a major industrial, cultural and transport centre. The new post-War borderline pushed it off the main routes, thus ending the town's administrative career. In the 1970s, owing to a national administration reform, it regained its former rank of voivodship capital – albeit, only for the next two decades.

Przemyśl is, above all, an urban complex unaffected by War-time damages – a rare quality in a country that was 30-percent ruined during the last War. Thus, naturally, the original Przemyśl has not been deformed by modern architecture. "A flesh-and-blood town" – as some like to call it. Its unavoidable modern expansion began recently across the River San, with the building of a new housing development, designed by Oskar Hansen, a disciple of Le Corbusier: it provoked controversial opinions.

Fourteen kilometres from Przemyśl, a new, busy railway with a traffic border pass to the Ukraine has been opened, which – considering all the recent political changes – has imposed a new role on the town.

Wieliczka

It lies in the immediate neighbourhood of Kraków, in fact, just beyond the city toll-gates. Wieliczka salt mines have been excavated since the 12th, or even the 10th century. Its underground vaults contain salt-chiselled 17th-century chapels. Although similar subterranean sanctuaries can be visited elsewhere in the world (including South American Columbia), Wieliczka seems to possess a unique character. A famous 17th-century French heraldist, Le Laboureur, wrote: "The salt mines at Wieliczka are as exceptional as the Egyptian pyramids, and much more useful. They offer a valuable proof of the Polish people's laboriousness, while the pyramids had been the fruit of the Egyptians' vanity and tyranny."

The baedekers give Wieliczka a triple star in their rankings. In 1978, it was included on the UNESCO list of World Cultural Heritage.

The eight excavation levels of the Wieliczka mines reach 315 metres into the earth. The joint length of all the underground chambers, galleries and corridors is 150 kilometres. At 50–100 metres below ground level are the famous salt chapels of St. Anthony (chiselled in 1675 by a local miner, Kuczkiewicz), the Holy Cross (with a 17th-century salt crucifix), St. Kinga (the length if this chapel is 54 metres), and others. At the depth of 135 metres, there is a musem of ancient tools and appliances, including a 16th-century mechanism allowing for vertical transport.

Among the treasures of this officially acclaimed natural reservation are the Crystal Caves – world-unique geological formations with halite crystals of unequalled beauty.

In the chamber named "Warszawa," 125 metres below the ground, dancing balls and tennis tournaments have been organised. During the War, a factory of spare aircraft parts had been installed by the Germans just below. The salt-mine also offers a sanatorium for patients with bronchitis, opened in 1964.

Wieliczka has hosted a number of Polish and foreign royal visitors, such as the Polish King Kazimierz the Great,

the German Emperor Sigismundus, or the Danish King Eric. Among its other eminent guests was Johann Wolfgang Goethe. Nowadays, Wieliczka receives 300 thousand tourists a year.

The salt-mines have often been endangered by leaking water – a powerful enemy that is being bravely fended off. Surprisingly, perhaps, salt had been excavated in Wieliczka until as late as 1996.

Wilanów

Opinions are divided on what King Jan III Sobieski's major historical contribution was: defeating the Turks at Vienna, or building the palace at Wilanów. Whatever the answer, while the echoes of the Viennese Campaign resound throughout the annals of history, the wonderful Wilanów Palace in Warsaw stands there, a "living object," for everyone to admire.

The residence of the Vienna hero who used to hunt herons in the rushes overgrowing the Vistula banks, is certainly worth visiting. The palace that had once been home to the King and his beloved French wife Maria, called Marysieńka, is now opened to the public. You can feel some of the old melancholy of this refuge, hidden among the mists and the rustling trees.

Wilanów Palace is among the most beautiful examples of Baroque architecture. Along with the park, it has been classified "zero" category in the international art catalogue. It is a building of exquisite harmony, perfect proportions and unique atmosphere. A tourist Mecca since 1962, when the last traces of the War-time damage were erased, Wilanów is a branch of the National Museum in Warsaw. It offers, among other things, the galleries of Polish portrait painting and Polish modern sculpture.

The estate used to belong to the noble families of, successively, Milanowski, Lubomirski, Czartoryski, Potocki and Branicki. The magnate residence was given a new shape at the end of the 17th century, by a group of famous artists headed by the Italian architect Augustino Locci, commissioned by the King. The interior decorators were sculptors Andrew Schluter and S. Szwaner, and painters Michel Angelo Palloni, Claude Callot and Jerzy Szymonowicz-Siemiginowski. In the later years, the palace was further decorated by G. Spazzio, Jacob Fontana, Christian Peter Aigner and Henryk Marconi.

The palace gives an impression of being lived-in, which amazes all its visitors. The rooms are amply and tastefully furnished. There are always fresh flowers in the vases, and the clocks duly measure the time. It seems that Queen Marysieńka is just about to appear in the doorway...

The palace entrance is topped with a golden Sun, glittering its many pointed beams. *"Refulsit Sol in clipeis"* – "The Sun has shone in the shields" – runs the inscription. And it never stops shining.

Wiślica

Towns are like people: they have their ups and downs. Wiślica lost its municipal rights long ago, but it must have been once a major centre of the Slav territory. An early-Medieval castle-town, it remained, until the end of the 10th century, a castellany and the seat of the local administrator. For a short time during the 12th century, it had been the capital of an independent dukedom in the Nida Valley.

Today's Wiślica is a sleepy village on the Nida River bank, surrounded by a gloomy marshland. Fourteen kilometres away is Busko Zdrój, and much closer – the station of the narrow-gauge railway connecting Kazimierza Wielka and Pińczów. There was a moment in Wiślica's recent past when its population became reduced

to 260 souls and it seemed that the place was doomed to become a typical ghost-town. Fortunately, this did not happen.

The village offers a number of truly metropolitan-size historic monuments. The main one is the 14th-century collegiate church, with the remnants of Russ-Byzantine polychromes and a memory plaque featuring King Kazimierz the Great.

Some truly sensational discoveries have been made since the War. Archaeological research revealed two rotundas and a few rectangular, brick buildings, one of them the duke's palace. It is supposed that Wiślica may have had been the centre of a Wiślanie state at the turn of the 10th century. This would make Poland a hundred years older than it is presently believed to be, on the basis of the existing documents.

In 1958, remains of an early 13th-century double-towered Romanesque façade were excavated, and lifting the floor revealed fragments of a 12th-century Romanesque church and crypt, including supportsof the columns and a gypsum floor with an engraved, black-mass-filled design featuring two groups of three. The floor is Poland's unique specimen of kind. Other precious discoveries included: a Gothic belfry built for Jan Długosz and the foundations of the one-aisle St. Michael's Church (c.10th–12th) with an apse, a quadrilateral chamber and a circular basin that may have been the baptismal font of the late 10th century.

And all that happened more than a hundred years after Wiślica was deprived of municipal rights. Some turn of fate, indeed.

The Choochoos

Narrow-gauge trains, more popular by their onomatopoeic nickname of choochoos, are still used in some regions of Poland, offering a welcome tourist attraction. Most of the narrow-gauge railways were built in the 19th century, to transport passengers and merchandise. The first narrow-gauge line in Poland was opened in 1853, in Upper Silesia. Those earliest trains had been pulled by horses which were later (in 1872) replaced with little steam engines.

Despite the general modernization that has replaced most of the puffing choochoos with new means of transport, quite a few have survived, not only in the outskirts of Poland, but also closer to the country's centre. The Central Board of State Railways in Warsaw still maintains its Commuter Train Management section.

A few choochoos continue to run on schedule, but the rest have become tourist attractions and are used only during the summer season.

Most of them are, of course, freight trains, transporting timber from the forests.

The width of a narrow-gauge railways is not uniform, ranging from 600, 750 or 785, to 1000 milimetres.

You may travel on a narrow gauge train between, e.g.: Sochaczew – Wilcze Tułowskie (18km.) Ełk – Turowo (38km.) Nowy Dwór Gdański – Malbork (33km.) Gryfice – Trzebiatów (55km.) Przeworsk – Dynów (46km.) and Hajnówka – Osada Topiło (12km). There are many more lines to try. In Sochaczew, Wenecja (a town in Greater Poland, though it bears the famous Italian name) and in Gryfice, there are museums of narrow-gauge railways.

The choochoo tracts often traverse picturesque landscapes that are hardly accessible otherwise. Through forest thickets and secluded villages and towns – especially in some parts of Mazury and Pomorze – goes the brave little engine, puffing away.

Travelling on an narrow-gauge train is like stepping behind the curtain of a strange theatre.

The Biebrza Marshland

Poland's largest marshland, and one of the largest in Europe, spreads in the river-valley of the Biebrza, a tributary of the Narew.

The estimated 45-hectare area of the Biebrza river basin contains the largest of the eight Polish marshlands. Beavers are raised in Osowiec, while Czerwone Bagno [Red Bog] is the natural habitat of elks. Other marshland animal species include: deer, wild boars, otters, foxes, skunks, martens, badgers and wolves. The rich and varied local vegetation is typical of marshland and turf areas. It is a birds' paradise: of the 235 bird species that inhabit the area, 157 nest in the neighbourhood, including a number of predators, such as the eagle, the osprey or the eagle-owl, while 21 other species have become almost extinct outside Biebrza: one of them is the runner – a bird that is capable of imitating various sounds, such as the squeaking of a frightened pig, the thumping of feet, or the plop of an uncorked bottle. The Biebrza River is home to 35 fish and lamprey species.

Following World War II, a drainage project was started in the Biebrza Marshland: though it has not been fully carried out, some irreparable damage has been done. The "experts" were not put off by the catastrophic effects of draining the nearby marshes of Polesie and went ahead with the project, partly draining the vast turfland at Kuwasy, east of Grajewo.

In 1993, the Biebrza Marshland was promoted to the rank of a National Park; the opening ceremony gathered many foreign celebrities, including the Dutch Prince Bernhard.

First settlers came to the Marshland a mere 400 years ago. Nowadays, Biebrza National Park has 690 inhabitants.

Zamość

In all baedekers, the entire town of Zamość is considered a historical monument, just like Carcassonne, or Padua. Indeed, one of the chief builders of Zamość was Bernardo Morando of Padua.

Zamość is a treasure of international rank. Founded on the classic principles of Renaissance architecture, it was for years a powerful stronghold that resisted many a siege and invasion. For two hundred years, it was home to the famous Zamojski Academy.

The vast area of the Grand Marketplace and its surroundings make up a top-(international)class architectural unit. On its northern side is the stately Town-hall (c.17th) built in mannerist style, with a characteristic, graceful tower. It is surrounded by many arcaded tenements. The collegiate church of St. Thomas (c.16th) is one of the finest examples of Polish Renaissance architecture. A constant struggle is waged to preserve all that has so luckily survived from the past. Zamość was the only Polish town that resisted the Swedish "deluge" of the 17th century. It also withstood the eight-months' siege of 1813, during the Napoleonic wars. During the last War, the occupants turned it into a city of cruel terror, murdering 8 thousand people in the Rotunda and killing even more in the many executions. The mass displacements of entire village populations in the years 1942–1943 shocked public opinion, as 293 out of the 696 local settlements were completely evacuated. Many of the DPs and deportees were Zamość children. Germanization attempts were strong all over the region.

Nowadays, modernity has reached even that antique-shop that is Zamość. More and more new housing developments are being built around the old town. The automobile-and-coffee-express civ-

ilization has entered Zamość, bringing swarms of cars to the parking lots and crowds of tourists to the ultra-modern café that has opened at the ground-floor of the Town-hall.

The famous Zamość also boasts a branch of Lublin Marie Curie-Skłodowska University, and a zoo of a many years' tradition. Indeed, the decision to build an opera house or an international airport in Zamość would be by no means a surprising one.

In 1989, after many decades when entry to the town was forbidden all those bearing the name of Zamoyski, a son of the last proprietor was elected mayor of the town.

admirer of the country manor on the bank of the Utrata (54 kilometres from Warsaw.) Żelazowa Wola has inspired many more literature, all melancholy. It is one of those few places "far from the madding crowd" that encourage a quiet reflection.

The park surrounding the manor is truly beautiful. Founded in 1935, thanks to the donations coming from all over the country, it contains several thousand plant species, many of them rare.

Żelazowa Wola

Frédéric Chopin was born here on 22 February, 1810. The small 18th-century country manor house contains a modest museum with blueprints of documents, as well as portraits and period furniture – there is a special atmosphere of the cult surrounding the genius composer. Sunday concerts of eminent Polish and foreign pianists are organized in the drawing room, the public crowding in the surrounding park to listen to the mazurkas and the preludes through the open windows. The concerts are held annually, from the last Sunday of May, until the last Sunday before 17 October (the date of the composer's death in 1849.) A poet once came here, on a week-day, when the place was not teeming with visitors...

The old spinet, the old manor,
I've got something in C-Major
(just a trifle, dear Sir)
an old song in the old scores,
now it's Autumn, the leaf falls.
Why, you're leaving? What a shame.
Goodness me, so far away!
Sir, your gloves. Oh, merci bien.
Bon soir, Monsieur Chopin.

The poet, Konstanty Ildefons Gał-czyński, was not the only literary

The Biebrza National Park, the "Ławki" Bog

The Traffic

In the "holy war" between the horse and the automobile, the latter was obviously the winner. Cartwheels have been replaced by Fiat and VW wheels. And yet, on many Polish roads – especially in the east – you will still meet a horse-and-cart – the driver's nightmare, especially if he happens to be a foreign driver, the shaft of a cart being more threatening than the devil's horns. But the shafts become fewer and fewer each year.

Polish traffic rules honour all the major international traffic regulations, but there are certain local variations and, of course, the drivers' habits. Formally, the traffic is right-side but, since all Polish drivers are continually taking over other cars, or preparing to do so, it may sometimes appear to follow the British, left-side model.

Naturally, all drivers willing to switch from a side-road to a main road must observe the right of way. But watch out for impatient local drivers who may not give you the chance to be such a law-abiding automobilist: driving along principal Polish motorways may bring some nasty surprises.

Polish people behind the wheel have a tendency to manifest a certain tension and agitation. Try to smile when they honk to urge you on, utter nasty comments, or make meaningful gestures around their foreheads.

A great majority of roads, even the local ones, have strengthened (albeit often uneven) surfaces and a good traffic sign system. However, to make the journey less monotonous, there may be an occasional deep hole in an otherwise smooth motorway, which, when spotted just in front of the car, will wake up even the most bored motorist.

The number of cars in Poland has been growing at avalanche speed. The many road accidents do not seem to spell enough warning to reckless drivers. Cities and, occasionally, open motorways, are plagued by traffic-jams. In Warsaw, the million locally registered cars and the continuous renovations of bridges and roads, make the city rather hard to drive around. Bicycles are highly recommended!

Car Stealing

Yes, it is true that cars are often stolen in Poland. According to an opinion propagated in some European countries, Polish car-thieves are unequalled masters of their trade. In fact, however – with all due respect to our foreign Readers – competition in the business is strong and the Poles are far from being monopolists in the car-stealin business.

In 1966, the number of cars stolen in Poland was 62,735, while the respective statistics reported 170,041 stolen cars in Germany, 342,625 in France and 98,847 in Spain.

Of course, there are more cars in Germany or in France, than there are in Poland, and the international gangs (of Poles, as well as Germans and Russians) have been active in many countries. But it is also a fact that the so-called "law-abiding citizens" in Germany, Holland or Switzerland are often the instigators of the thefts that allow them to collect high compensations from insurance companies.

The Climate

"It's a mild winter we've been having this summer" – runs a new Polish proverb. People have been complaining about changes in the climate that have brought wet and snowless winters, while the summers have become rainy and chilly. Could it be the Black Hole? If it were not for the global changes in our climate, those complaints might be put down to an ungrounded pessimism. It is true, however, that the routine of the four seasons has slackened down over the last decades, turning the popular saying: "Carry your umbrella when the sun shines, too" into a sound piece of advice. This may also explain an increasing inaccuracy of the weather forecasts.

Poland's average annual temperature (except in the mountains) is 6–8.8°C. The mean temperature in July reaches 16.5–19°C, while in January it drops to 0–4.5°C. The number of days with temperatures below 0°C is between 23 and 65, depending on the region. The average rainfall is 600mm, with 1200–1500mm in the mountains.

A specific characteristic of the Polish climate is its changeability. Temperatures may vary by up to 20°C within 24 hours.

So – carry your umbrella when the sun shines, too.

Polish Hell

Americanization of the Polish people has become a fact. The same is true about the rest of Europe, and a great part of the other continents. But there will always remain certain Polish characteristics that I have mentioned earlier in this book: a Pole says "thank you" when leaving the table, complains about life in general while talking to a friend, kisses ladies on the hand and brings them flowers.

There are more typically Polish qualities, some of them quite important. In everyday social relations, the Poles are less spontaneous and less cheerful than the Americans. They are not inclined towards excessive friendliness. But they treat friendship with great seriousness. The Polish people celebrate their namesdays, rather than birthdays – yet, they do not ignore a person's age, which is evidenced by the popularity of "Sto lat" ["May He Live a Hundred Years"] – a song wrongly believed by some foreigners to be the Polish national anthem.

The ceremony of breaking the Wafer at Christmas Eve is still popularly observed, as is the custom of sharing the Easter Egg, after it has been consecrated in church: both are occasions to exchange good wishes.

Polish people have never been masters of reliability and punctuality. The present troublesome traffic in many cities gives them a new, ideal excuse for being late.

Bureaucracy is thriving in Poland. The average Pole is involved in relations with many administrative organisations with whom he exchanges an active correspondence, in the meantime spending long hours in office corridors and waiting rooms. This makes him irritable and prone to fits of anger.

The Pole gossips and is the object of gossip. He makes sarcastic comments about other people, certain that they do the same about himself. Everybody believes himself to be the sole victim of the "Polish hell."

The Language

What language do the Polish speak? An extremely difficult one, full of hisses, shshes and tschtschs. To make things worse, the Polish written language includes some letters unknown in other alphabets, namely: ą, ę, ł, ż, ź, ć, ś, ń and dż; some of its sounds have a double notation (e.g. [u] being written as "u" or "ó"), and certain combinations of letters have pronunciations that defy the foreign common sense, such as: "ch" [h], rz [zh], sz [sh], or cz [tsch].

The Polish language belongs to the West-Slavonic group of Indo-European languages. It is presently spoken by some 50 million people in Poland and abroad. Polish vocabulary is estimated at 120 thousand words, the average intellectual employing about 10 thousand – though, when you listen to some young people in the street, it sounds more like a hundred. The recorded history of the Polish language begins in 1136, with the so-called "Gniezno Bull" of Pope Innocent II. Polish literary language flourished in the mid-16th century, gradually replacing the fading charms of Latin that had been the language of the literate, i.e. the clergy, the court officials and some of the gentry.

Like many other languages of the world, the Polish national language has often been an object of persecution: there have been times when speaking or writing Polish could send a person to prison.

A modern problem with Polish – felt also by the French and the Italians – is the growing number of foreign borrowings in the vocabulary, most of them American. Home-bred neologisms also provoke many controversies. On the other hand, the accent has become more homogeneous, as many local dialects have been gradually neutralized.

Polish is a living and changing language, which may be observed during meetings with the Polish emigrants: those who left Poland more than 30 years ago will not understand many words, while some words they use will not be comprehended by a modern Polish citizen. A specific dialect is spoken by the Polish-born-several-generations-American citizens: they use a "Polamerican" pidgin language, combining American-English vocabulary with the Polish grammar.

Foreign visitors to Poland try to master some basic words and expressions, such as: ile [ile] = how much, dokąd [dokont] = where to; panie [panie] = ladies; panowie [panovie] = gentlemen; prosze dać [proshe dat'] = please, give; pani jest śliczna [pani iest slit na] = you are lovely; nie, nie mam dolarów [nie, nie mam dolaruv] = no, I have no dollars. The rules of Polish conjugation get easier, once you have mastered the pattern of "I love you/ you love me/ he loves you" (ja cię kocham; ty mnie kochasz; on cię kocha...)

Unlike in Britain, neither a *Lover's Dictionary* for womanizers, nor a *Dictionary of Insults* (with phrases like "Keep your hands to yourself, you swine!" or "Pass an extra plate for the vermine") have been published in Poland, so you have to fend for yourself.

The Author of this book has had the

dubious pleasure of being greeted abroad by a gallant English gentleman with a bunch of the most filthy Polish swear-words of whose meaning the innocent speaker was perfectly ignorant. It turned out that the gentleman had picked them up during the War, while fighting the Battle of Britain shoulder to shoulder with the brave Polish airmen.

Those who have absolutely no gift for learning languages are advised to stick to places advertising their services in the fashion of a certain cinema that promised: "No dialogues, much shooting!" Films of this kind are becoming more and more popular in Poland

Polish Cuisine

Maria Iwaszkiewicz, the distinguished daughter of the writer Jarosław, tells the readers in the Preface to her cookery book:

"*Why am I writing about food? What has given me the idea? Well, it all began with an irritating observation that the culinary art is declinig, perishing.*" The author expertly and gracefully proceeds with a compilation of Polish cooking recipes, doing all she can to preserve the traditions, if only in theory.

Deploring the decline of national cuisines is not a monopoly of the Polish. It has become a global phenomenon, enhanced by the American-style gastronomy that has suppressed the inventiveness of the local masters of the pot and pan. Everybody is in a hurry, our palates are becoming less and less subtle, and the instant soups and beef-steaks are so cheap and so easy to prepare... MacDonald's has eliminated Mum's Cooking.

Following several decades of state-owned bars and restaurants, serviced by state-employed bureaucrat-gastronomers, the businesses have now been privatized, which means that everything – except for the prices – is back to the normal.

A number of delicious dishes have been invented in the country on the Vistula. Some can be eaten everyday, while others are prepared for special occasions, such as Christmas, Ash Wednesday, the carnival, Easter, or New Year's Eve (a special pudding).

Polish specialities include: red borscht with "ear" dumplings, hunter's stew (believed to be best after it has been kept in the larder for two weeks,) dumplings with various fillings (cottage cheese and potatoes, minced meat, or wild mushrooms,) pickled *Lactarius deliciosus* mushrooms,

poppy-seed yeast cake, etc. Meat is traditionally cooked as: hussar's roast, T-bone pork steak with cabbage, mutton Polish style, beef chops with buckwheat, or roast duck with apples.

Follow the old Polish saying: "Eat, drink, and loosen your belt."

Tips for Travellers

"Poland especially lacks inns and hostels where one could find a comfortable accommodation with a bed."

This observation was made in the 17th century, by a French nobleman, de Hauteville, travelling across Poland. Three and a half centuries later, it cannot be denied that the problem still exists. The growing number of foreign tourists, as well as the increasing mobility of the local citizens, render the country's developing tourist base insufficient. In 1997, Poland received 19.8 million tourists, which makes it the eighth most visited country in the world. Reality may be hard, and therefore a traveller to Poland must be cunning like a fox, sturdy and self-reliant. The number of hotels has been growing especially fast in big cities, like Warsaw, Poznań, Kraków, Wrocław, Lublin, Toruń, or Bydgoszcz. But smaller towns and villages have also started building new hotels. Alas, most of the newly-built hotels are five and four-star palaces, while the demands of tourists with thinner wallets are being ignored.

A prudent traveller (not only to Poland) will book a hotel room before setting out on the journey. However, early reservations must be regularly checked and confirmed, as they sometimes tend to vanish into thin air.

Monsieur de Hauteville had survived in Poland thanks to the help of the local people – we are still known to be a hospitable nation. Monsieur's modern followers may have some trouble finding a bed in a hotel, but they will never lack help and friendliness.

Luckily, the times are now past when a traveller to Poland was wholly dependent on those qualities. He need not any longer take a kind word instead of fuel for his car, since filling stations (selling the unleaded, too) are in great supply. Neither is friendliness any longer a substitute for a smooth road, a convenient airplane connection, a money exchange office (though in this respect local people still try to offer their own services,) a car-hire, or a souvenir shop.

Some time ago, the owner of a big Western tourist agency complained that "Poland doesn't sell well." There is still some truth in this statement.

After all, Poland for many years ignored the tourist industry, largely due to the political xenophobia of the communist authorities – though not of the citizens. It sounds like prehistory today.

Poland has never been a tourist shop-window. Despite its many unique attractions, the country's uniqueness is not in its historic monuments and art treasures. And as for the climate, it is not quite your Italy, either. The secret lies in the sense of adventure that you get while wandering around Poland – more intense, perhaps, than in any other modern European country. The feeling may be sometimes slightly disquieting, but it is so welcome!

Some More or Less Useful Statistics

Poland has 212 monastic congregations, with nearly 40 thousand monks and nuns. They run orphanages, schools, kindergartens, homes for single mothers, for the disabled, the elderly and the homeless, hospices and clinics – as well as publishing houses and bookshops.

In summer 1998, the popular *Wprost* magazine published a ranking of Polish academies, including 94 state and 183 private ones. Their total is probably the present number of academies in Poland. Among the 18 classified by *Wprost* as schools of international rank were: Warsaw University, the Main School of Commerce in Warsaw, Jagiellonian University in Krakow and State Academy of Film, Television and Theatre in Łódź. The ranking did not include the European University in Frankfurt on the Oder – a research and study centre of international importance.

International Poznań Fairs are no longer a monopoly enterprise. Apart from Poznań, major commercial events have been regularly organised in 19 other Polish towns, including Katowice, Warsaw, Gdańsk, Kielce, Wrocław, Krakow, Łódź, Bydgoszcz and Szczecin. More and more foreigners have been byuing land in Poland. In 1997, 2001 permissions were issued, concerning the sales of nearly 3 thousand hectares – 500 hectares more than in the previous year – to foreign owners, mostly German, Dutch, American and Swedish. The area presently leased to foreigners is estimated at 150-200 thousand hectares, plus a large number of apartments.

Poland is the storks' favourite European country. When spring comes, in some villages there are more storks than people.

Contents

GRAPHICS BY
Janusz Kapusta

PHOTOGRAPHS BY
Jan Morek 5, 22-23, 25, 29, 30, 31, 36-37, 41, 47, 48, 50-51, 52-53,
54, 55, 56-57, 60, 61, 62-63, 64-65, 67, 68-69, 70-71, 72, 73, 74-75,
76, 77, 78, 79, 80-81, 82-83, 84-85, 86, 87, 88-89, 90, 91, 92-93, 94,
95, 96-97, 98, 100-101, 102, 108-109, 112, 116, 118-119, 120-121,
122, 123, 124-125, 126-127, 128, 129, 132, 133, 136, 137, 142,
144-145, 146, 147, 155
Jan Słodowski 38, 39, 40, 42-43, 44-45, 46, 58-59, 66, 103, 105, 107,
115, 117, 130-131, 134-135, 143, 148-149
Agencja Piękna: Ryszard Czerwiński 114, Cezary Krywiczanin 113,
Maciej Musiał 110, Piotr Płaczkowski 49, Tadeusz Sumiński 99,
Beata Tomaszewska 11, 111, Mieczysław Wieliczko 106, 138,
Wiesław Mariusz Zieliński 104, 139, 140-141
Archiwum WAiF 33, 55

Wydawnictwa Artystyczne i Filmowe
REDACTOR IN CHIEF
Janusz Fogler

LAYOUT
Maciej Buszewicz

EDITING
Joanna Słodowska, Artibus

TECHNICAL ASSISTANCE
Janusz Kopacz, TAK

LAYOUT EXECUTION
Wojciech Szombara

SET OF PRINT BY
Artgraph, Warschau

PRINTED BY
Zakłady Graficzne ATEXT S.A., Gdańsk

© Copyright by Wydawnictwa Artystyczne i Filmowe, Warszawa 2000
Design and layout © copyright Maciej Buszewicz 2000

ISBN 83-221-0706-4
ISBN 83-01-13059-8

This book has been published with financial assistance
from Warsaw Municipal Council

some of the objects of interest dispersed off the main traffic areas, such as the Baroque and Classicist palaces in Krasińskich Square, in Miodowa and Senatorska streets, in Bankowy Square, or in Puławska Street. Moving chess-knigt-like across the city, you will pass the Cameldolite church in Bielany district, Królikarnia in Puławska Street, the Ghetto Monument, and the Evangelical Mosque in Kredytowa Street.

A surprising edifice is Lubomirski Palace, closing the main prospect of Saski Gardens and bridging the gap between two modern blocks of flats. On older maps of Warsaw (before 1970), the palace has a different situation, perpendicular to the traditionally popular market of Hala Mirowska. Has it been wandering around?

Yes, the Neoclassicist Lubomirski Palace has been shifted to a new location. Between 30 March and 18 May, 1970, the then 250 years old, 10-thousand-ton edifice was moved along 16 rails, not a single brick of the main bulk being displaced in the operation. It was turned round by 78 degrees. Thus, the old palace amazed the Varsavians, suddenly appearing at the crown of the axis cutting the green space of Saski Gardens, to face the Tomb of the Unknown Soldier.

However unusual, the translocation of Lubomirski Palace was not a unique incident of this kind in Warsaw: some years earlier, the Carmelite Church in Solidarność Avenue had been shifted backwards by 21 metres, and the position of the Grochów Toll-Gate had been changed – proving that it is not only the restorers of art who work wonders in Warsaw.

Though not the brightest pearl of Warsaw's architecture, the "palace on rollers" is certainly worth seeing.

So is the right-bank district of Praga, with its present population of 400 thousand – though it has never been a favourite with Warsaw tourist guides. Praga had been traditionally spoken of like a far-off, exotic land. Its "otherness" and "eastern-ness" were said to resemble cities lying some 300 and more kilometres east of the Vistula. It was perceived as a "kitchen door" to Warsaw.

It is only in the recent years that the opinion of Praga as an alienated suburb started losing its validity. The right-bank "continent" has been coming closer and closer to the city, taking over some of the capital's functions and imitating its appearance to acquire a more "European" style. Few people nowadays remember that Praga had had its own, distinct – mostly tragic – history and specific traditions. It is the only part of Warsaw where you may still observe the remains of the local lumpenproletariat and the all-but-extinct Jewish folklore. Praga has its traditional bazaars, the "immortal" Różycki Bazaar being the largest one, as well as wooden tenant houses and narrow streets, some of them paved with cobblestone; its centre is marked by the onion-shaped roofs of the Orthodox church.

We may be living in the last years of Praga district's uniqueness. All over its vast area, wooden tenements are being replaced with clusters of soaring highrises.

The transformations in Praga are no longer part of Warsaw's post-War reconstruction: they are a "change of skin," a usual stage in the rather rapid development of the city.

The busy traffic of the central Marszałkowska Street is dominated by the 230-metre-high bulk of the Palace of Culture and Science – originally dedicated to Joseph Stalin, it is a virtual "city within a city," with an inside area of 13 hectares. The often ridiculed Palace has never been popular with Warsaw citizens, though many for-

eigners find it impressive. Following the overall systematic changes, this giant edifice is also undergoing major functional transformations. Its interiors have been occupied by dozens of companies and institutions, both national and international.

The Palace of Culture's immediate neighbour is Warsaw Central Station, serving 100 thousand passengers each day. Even though the statistics of local petty thieving have never been published, travellers are advised to mind their pockets in this area.

Following the results of a recent competition, the neighbourhood of the Palace of Culture will be changed, its vast surrounding wasteland built over to screen the now dominant architectural element of the city-scape. Preparatory works for the realization of the winner project are already under way. Meanwhile, the area has been occupied by an army of petty tradesmen, whose activity is slowly being limited.

The recent years have brought a number of changes in Warsaw's topography. There are more and more banks, hotels and modern-style international companies' quarters. Those glittering cathedrals of modern civilisation have transformed the city-scapes of Warsaw's "wild west" (i.e. Wola district.) its City (with the historic Town-hall reconstructed by two banking companies in Teatralny Square) and the suburbs. The construction of the underground is also proceeding.

We may well quote the opinon of Irving Brandt, a special reporter of the "Chicago Sun," who informed from Poland's capital just after the War: "Upon arriving in Warsaw, an American feels as if he had been extracted from real life and dumped in the midst of a world that seems too fantastic to be true."

How much has changed in this city during the lifetime of one generation!

Warsaw Neighbourhood

Within 60 kilometres from Warsaw, there are some truly interesting spots, although, generally, the area cannot be called beautiful – Kampinoska Forest and the Zegrze Reservoire being just two welcome exceptions to the rule. Nevertheless, the palace and park of Wilanów in Warsaw suburbs, built for King Jan III Sobieski, is ranked among the most beautiful magnate residences in Central Europe. And nobody will deny that it is worthwhile to visit the Palace in Jabłonna, built by Domenico Merlini for Polish and French Marshal Prince Józef Poniatowski, or to take a 30-plus-kilometre trip to the south, to stand and ponder in the shade of the 15th-century ruin of the giant Gothic castle of Czersk – one-time residence of the Mazovian Princes, lords of this county.

The region called Mazowsze, whose centre has traditionally been in Warsaw, had always been densely populated, albeit poor, lacking fertile soils and mineral resources, overgrown with wild forests and pestered by enemy attacks from the north. Consequently, its social and economic development was retarded.

But the peculiar charm of the region is not to be found in great works of art, or in special tourist attractions, but, rather, in a slightly melancholy, relfexive mood that you discover while walking up the Vistula escarpment in nearby Góra Kalwaria to get a broad view of the peaceful, green, bucolic landscape beneath. The same, inimitably Mazovian tune is promptly discovered in a stylish country manor house in Żelazowa Wola – the birthplace of one of the most illustrious Polish citizens and world's artists: Frédéric Chopin.

Warsaw is surrounded by considerably vast areas of forest. Apart from

Kampinoska Forest (which is a national park) that spreads over 21,894 hectares of the land, there are several other major woods: Chotomowskie, Kabackie, Sękocińskie, Chojnowskie, etc. Neither is the River Vistula, crossing the centre of the Warsaw Valley, the only "big water" in the region: the considerably small area is also saturated by the Narew, the Bug, the Bzura, the Pilica, the Liwiec, the Wkra, the Rządza and the Świder – some of them big and dangerous, while others hardly waist-deep for a child. Less than 30 kilometres from Warsaw is the Zegrzyński Reservoir, built in 1963 by cutting off the river-bed of the Narew with the dam at Dębe.

Warsaw neighbourhood is easiest penetrated by car, the roads being generally acceptable, and nearly all the city outlets having been conveniently modernized. However, as seasoned travellers say, it is better to view the world from the donkey's back than from a plane, and therefore we advise walking trips. It is a pity, though, that the suburban narrow-gauge trains – the funny choo-choos, also known as the "Blue Express" – are no longer in use in Warsaw area.

The Warsaw – Krakow Route

The 300-kilometre route may well be called Poland's principal promenade. Over the centuries, it has been trampled along by national and foreign armies. It was also – between Wieliczka and Krakow – part of the most important merchant route, leading from Hungary to the Baltic Coast. And, not far from Krakow, it crossed the major Kiev – Lvov – Prague road. Its popularity began with the first recorded foreign globetrotter-trader's visit to Poland: in the 10th century, Ibrahim Ibn Jakub arrived from Spain, to continue his journey south from Warsaw to Prague. In his report, the reverend Ibrahim remarked:

"I have journeyed across a beautiful and exceptional country, whose people do not confine themselves solely to the martial arts, but also send their products abroad, by land and water, to Russia and to Constantinople."

For a thousand years, the areas along the Vistula banks had been scenes of major political, economic and cultural changes. They are dotted with Gothic, Renaissance and Baroque architecture, both secular and sacral, of great value and beauty – from antique wooden sanctuaries and synagogues, down to historic town-halls and magnate palaces.

This is the Poland that had charmed so many great artists. The Mazovian willows rustle in the nocturnes of Frédéric Chopin, as do the fir trees of the Świętokrzyskie Mountains in the novels of Stefan Żeromski.

The foundations of the Polish state were set in the areas of Wiślica and Krakow. And many relics of the ancient cultures have been discovered in the neighbourhood of Kielce. The two supporting pillars of the historic trail are Warsaw and Krakow: the present, and the former capitals of the country.

Though permeated with modern civilisation, this region of Europe still holds something of the aura of the times long past. You may come across living examples of timeless folk traditions, and oases of unpolluted landscape.

Krakow